**Dedicated
Gran & Gramp
Ada & George Parrish
& my husband Mike
Without their love, understanding &
support, I would not be who I am today.**

Contents

Dawn Griffis nee' Alsford

I was born, raised and educated in rural England, mainly in Aynhoe and Oxford. I also did most of my nurses training at the Horton General Hospital in Banbury, Oxfordshire.

I recently retired from nursing, after fifty years, which has enabled me to work on finishing this book, which I started over thirty years ago. I have almost completed a second book - "Nursing at the Horton - The Way It Was – When Care to the Local People Really Mattered". I started that over twenty years ago.

I have been married to Mike for almost 45 years, and we have two daughters - Jane and Penny plus six grandchildren.

Mike and I have lived and worked, in many regions of the United States. Those experiences have led to a third book - "Nursing and Living in America – The Way It Was – The Good, The Bad and The Ugly."

We returned to our beloved England in 2005, after almost forty years in the States. I continued to work in Nursing, until I finally retired in 2006.

8

Acknowledgements

I would like to say a thank you to the following people ,who have helped in the completion of this book. Though it has been many years in the making, the last year has been the most intense.

To those that have donated pictures: My late father, Sydney Alsford; My cousin Tony Parrish; My late Aunt Kath and Uncle Denis Parrish; My friend Edwin Bowerman, and David Morgan, who lives in Charlton. He supplied most of the Aynhoe School, and old village pictures. Also to Nigel Cartwright, for permission to use the photograph, of Julia Cartwright's painting of Aynhoe School, dated 1848.

To my grandparents, the late Ada and George Parrish, who were never too tired to tell me; "just one more story". Without their stories this book would be nothing; and also to the older villagers that would reminisce. To my sister and brother June and Norman Alsford they will often add; "Just one more story". To my mother, Norah Rouse who over the past year has added some additional stories, and clarification on others, plus several picture identifications.

To Ian Huckin, who over the past months has taught me so much; including how to put the book together; if necessary how to publish it myself, and to have it ready for the printers. Most especially his patience, with the many phone calls, when I could not make the computer do the things I wanted it to, and for the final proof reading.

To our daughters Jane Dandurand, Penny Gramling; grandchildren Reuben, Ruth – Ellen, Seth, Victoria Dandurand; Jason and Corey Gramling; they all gave me the reason to write this book initially, and encouraged me to do it for others to read. They have each refused to read it, until it is finished and published.

Finally to my husband Mike. A special thank you for his love, support, patience and guidance over these many years. Because of my type of dyslexia, he has re-read and corrected this book, more times than he or I care to remember. He has taught me to compensate and recognise my mistakes in advance, like no teacher ever did. I couldn't have completed it without him.

Dawn Griffis

Introduction

The first chapter is the only one that has the typical history information of a village. The rest of the book is more of what life was like during the different eras. It is centred around one house and the family that lived there. But, as anyone will know that has lived in a village, it is the whole village, and the villagers that makes life and survival there possible.

The 'Then' covers the wartime plus 3 years, 1940 to 1948, and what life was like during those difficult times. The 'Before' covers the years from 1880 ish to 1940. These are mainly stories about life in the village, as told by family members and other villagers. The 'Beyond' is from 1948 to 1956 - the post war years. It covers the changes that took place in the village life; of leaving, visiting frequently, and then returning there to live.

It is the type of social history that will be lost forever if not told, re-told, and written down, because memories are fickle. In light of fickle memories, if others reading this book remember a story differently; then please tell your family what you believe to be true. These stories are as they were told to me, and how I remember them. Maybe this book will encourage others to do the same, and tell about the places and people they love. Many of the older villagers that still live there, have helped me put names to faces in the old pictures. They are Edwin Bowerman, Sybil Stevens, Margaret Grant, Suzanne Neset, June & Norman Alsford, and Norah Rouse. If we have made errors and misnamed any I apologise. I have tried to leave enough space for names to be hand written in, of those that we missed.

For the genealogical readers, I hope seeing names of their ancestor makes them feel closer to them. In some instances, seeing photographs of Aynhoe in the years past, adds to what they learn of their antecedents, and the place where they lived.

Dawn

Chapter 1
Aynhoe

Aynhoe is a small village on the eastern edge of the Cotswolds, located at the southernmost tip in the county of Northamptonshire. It is six miles south of Banbury, and 19 miles north of Oxford. The village sits on the top of a hill, and is 565 feet above sea level. There is a marker stating this, on one of the houses in the village square.

There is recorded evidence, as to the existence of a village being there, in the time of Edward the Confessor. It was held in the King's name by a Saxon named Asgar in about 1043. It is reported that there was once a Norman Castle, stood on the site where Aynhoe Park House now stands. The Park House was the home of the Cartwright family, the village squire, for over 300 years, and had been destroyed by the Royalists at the end of the Civil War. It was restored in the 1680s.

Station Road now called Round Town

The name Aynhoe reportedly comes from either a Saxon landowner named Aeien or translated from the Saxon 'Aegas Hoh' (Aegas Spur), or spring on the Hill. The spelling has varied a lot over the centuries; Aienho in the Doomsday book, Eynho in the Book of Fees; The Episcopal Register has it as Ainho. Before the Second World War it was spelled Aynhoe, and then the post office changed it to Aynho. Now, officially, only the Park House uses the spelling Aynhoe. When it was first changed, the Park House would return all post, or would refuse to accept it, if it did not have the 'e' on it. The villagers should have done the same thing, and then maybe we would still have our 'e'. Some still prefer the pre-war spelling and continue to use it.

The original houses in the village were built from local limestone, and most were thatched. The oldest house in the village was built in the early 1500s; while most of the original village was built in the 1600s. The village has a host of listed buildings, which means they are historically protected, and the exteriors along the front cannot be changed.

There are many bridle paths that traverse the fields between the surrounding villages. There are also many natural springs in and around the village, so water has always been plentiful. These springs feed the numerous streams that run through or around the fields.

There is a Roman - British Road that edges the village on the eastern side called 'Portway '. There is also a Roman tunnel, that exits inside one of the houses on the northern edge of the village, that was an escape route for the Ro-  man soldiers stationed at Rainsborough Camp, a former Roman camp, one mile to the east of the village. All that remains of the camp, is the elevated fortified area, and the indention from the moat that surrounded it. There are traces of walls that were used to build the moat. I think it would be interesting to dig around in the area, to see what could be found, but then one would have to deal with a headless horseman that is supposed to frequent the place. My mother said It was just a tale the local farmers told, to keep the kids out; though one cannot be too sure about that. The escape tunnel entrance at the camp has, to my knowledge, never been locat- ed.

House on the corner Where Roman tunnel exits

Portway starts at Borough Hill near Daventry in Northamptonshire, and ends at Arncott, near Bicester, in Oxfordshire. There are burial sites, close to the line of the road near Aynhoe, that are suggestive of pre-his- toric origins. The road, as it passes through Aynhoe now, is really nothing more than a path. After crossing the Croughton road, it enters The Park House grounds over a stone stile, between high walls to pro- tect the privacy of the Park grounds. Portway used to be called First Crossing, with Second Crossing being further east opposite the Bicester Road, and to the left of the road that travels on to Croughton.

The houses in Portway Gardens, are on the site of the former pig fields. Across from these is where the limestone quarries were - this is where the stone came from to build the original houses in the village. The fields to the right and behind these, close to the village, were known as Big and Little Butts. So named because it was where the archers used to practice in preparation for forthcoming battles. At the corner of Portway and the Charlton Road (formerly called Brackley Road), on the other side, is a small spinney called Spion Kop. The trees were planted in commemoration of the Boer War battle of that name. It was in this same spinney that the gypsies camped during the 1940s. This area is at the top of Green Lane, and continues through to Walton Grounds.

Between Portway and Second Crossing are the village allotments. Beyond the Second Crossing are the Pest House woods, named after the house where people from the village were taken in the 1800's, if they had a contagious or an infectious disease. They would be isolated, to prevent the disease from spreading to the rest of the village. There was an old lady by the name of Mrs. Watts, who lived and worked there taking care of them. Food was taken from the village each day, and left at the end of the road to be collected by her. I am sure some got well and returned to the village. I am just as sure many died there, only to return to the village for burial. According to the 1881 census, her son, George Watts a gamekeeper, lived in the second house. The other house was listed as 'uninhabited'. Years later it was pulled down, and the stone was used to build the village hall. The village hall is very large, so the Pest House must have been a pretty good size too.

The village's high elevation, affords views into the Cherwell Valley from the north- western side. The valley is so named because of the River Cherwell, that runs through it on its way to Oxford. One road leads to Banbury, the other to Aynhoe Station, a mile away, and on to Deddington. The fields down the Station Road to the right, are relics of the medieval open field system, with evidence of Ridge and Furrow ploughing.

The field to the left is called Friar's Well. At one time the location of a monastery, it had been built adjacent to another spring. To the right is College Farm, so named because it was purchased by Magdalen College, Oxford in 1483. In the late 12th century the farm was a hospital. Called SS James and John Hospital at Aynhoe on the Hill. At the bottom of the first hill, down the Station Road, turn left into Miller's Lane.

Opposite there is another Green Lane. Miller's Lane leads to the Park House Lower Grounds. Lower Grounds was mostly off limits during the war years, as it housed holding tanks of fuel. The army built roads through the whole area. From the Lower Grounds the "Ha - Ha" can be seen. It protects the Park House gardens from the Park deer, without spoiling the view.

Continue to the end of Miller's Lane, and there is another bridle path to the Souldern Mill. The trout stream runs past the mill. If this is followed to the right it leads to the viaducts, and on to the River Cherwell and Oxford Canal, also known as the Cut. Under the viaducts the land is very boggy and isolated, so many interesting birds and plants can be found. Following the stream to the left at the mill, will take you through the bottom of Park Grounds, and will eventually come out on the Bicester Road. The going could be pretty tough through there, even for a healthy child back in the late nineteen-forties. If the path is taken straight up from Souldern Mill, it will lead into the village of Souldern.

G.W. Railway Station Aynhoe 1929

The second hill down Station Road, before the station and on the left, is a field called Common Hill. Villagers were allowed to use this field as common land, for their animals to graze. In the bottom of the valley, the Oxford Canal follows through. Nearby is the Great Western Railway, which travels from Paddington Station in London to Snow Hill in Birmingham. A little further on is the River Cherwell. There is a second railway line, which is the Princes Risborough Line to Marylebone in London. The sta-

Aynhoe Park Station   1927

16

tion for that was Aynhoe Park Station, so called because part of the track ran through Park land. Along the side of that station, there used to be a cattle market held each week. The brick buildings were still there when I was a child. Close to the main train station was a brickyard, where bricks were made using local clay. They were marked either AYNHOE or ABC. My Aunt Kath has one in her garden that is marked AYNHOE. In 1881 a Henry Wrighton ran the brickyard. He and his wife Julia (nee Borton) had 15 children.

Another important building in the same area, is the Great Western Arms. It is commonly known as 'the pub at the station'. In the late 1940's, this was a popular Sunday evening family walk from the village. I remember sitting outside on the grass bank, enjoying a lemonade drink and a bag of Smith's Crisps. On the way back, it was fun to look for any narrowboats that might be travelling along the canal. In 1881, a family called Howes ran the pub at the station. They had three children, one of which worked as a barmaid. They had three servants and one boarder - the Railway Station Master. Later the Station Masters had their own house right next to the station.

In the 1881 census, besides the land that was part of the Park holdings, there were private farms, varying in size from three to 712 acres. Most of these were owned by

The Square: old Post Office on the Rt. Wilkins off license facing. Eaton's Grocery shop far Lt

the farmer. The Cartwright Arms also operated a 415 acre farm.

In the centre of Aynhoe is the village square. Weekly markets were held there on Tuesdays from 1324 until the late 1700s. The square was the site of the annual Michaelmas Fair held every September 29th. The Posting House, on the edge of the square, was the site of the Bell Inn. It was rebuilt in the 16th century as the Red Lion. This backs onto Skittle Alley where skittles were played. The room above the archway was the room used by the Pig Club. Most villagers owned pigs, a practice that continued well into the 1950s. In the square was a Grocery Shop, a Butcher's Shop, a Post Office, and Off License. The village school was up a lane off of the square. Hollow's Road, or as it is now called Hollow Way, travels north off the square. It is a single track and used to be the main London to Birmingham Road. It was still the main road when my grandmother was a child, but that has long since been diverted around the village. There is an elevated pathway called the causeway. This is safer for pedestrians to walk on and it acts as a buttress against the gardens on the higher side of the hill. Halfway down Hollow Way, there is a wide path to the left leading to Hill cottages –

Causeway: Hollow Rd to Rt.
Blacksmith Hill to Lt.

most of which are still thatched.

A little further down there is a road to the right called Blacksmith's Hill. Just at the top of the hill, on the left, are the oldest cottages, formerly known as Pintle Row. Number 33 is reportedly the oldest and is dated c.1500. In the back of this house is the last exterior stone

The Causeway looking up Hollow Rd
Now called Holloway

staircase, which connected the bedroom to ground level. The tallest building in the village is next to it, and has mullioned windows. Skittle Alley comes out onto Blacksmith's Hill at this point.

There were three fairly large village greens as late as the 1940s. Now they are just a shadow of their former selves.

Village Green and Cartwright Arms 1920's

Most of the houses were thatched; many have been re-roofed in slate or tile. Those that were re-roofed, were able to have the walls raised, allowing for extra rooms, because slate and tile do not need as steep a pitch.

18

Aerial view of Aynhoe 1946

The village pub is called the Cartwright Arms, after the Squires family name. It is on one side of the village green, across from the village hall. There was a large solid gate, with a walk in door, that leads into the courtyard. The gate was purchased by the villagers. The walk in door was constructed, so people could walk through without having to open the large double gates, because a public footpath ran through it. The courtyard accommodated the horses and stagecoaches, that were used prior to motorised vehicles. There were stables at the back to house the horses, now used mainly for storage. There is a high wall along the right side, that allows privacy to the owner's garden. The courtyard is so large, that at the end of the war, on VE Day, they put two fighter planes in it for people to get a closer look at them.

Another building of interest in the village, is the Jacobean Grammar House. It was originally built as a Free Grammar School, established in 1654. It remained a school for well over two hundred years. In the 1881 census it was still functioning. The master was a Charles Davis from Abergavenny, Monmouthshire. He had a wife and a daughter listed as living there. Plus a governess, cook and housemaid, along with eleven male boarding students, and one female boarding student. She was probably a companion student for his daughter.

Aynhoe has eight Alms Houses. They were built in 1822, with a bequest from John Baker, an Oxford glazier. The story is told, that Mr. Baker was caught out in a blizzard, whilst traveling the bridle path between Kings Sutton and Aynhoe. He had completely lost his sense of direction, when the Aynhoe church bells rang out. He was able to walk in the direction of the bells to safety. He believed his life was saved by the sound of the bells. The residents of the Alms Houses, designated to be four poor men and four poor women of the village, were required to attend church twice on Sundays.

The village church is St. Michael's and All Angels. The original church was built during the reign of Edward III. The 14th century

19

tower is of the decorated period, with its embattled top. The body of the church received heavy damage during the civil war, and was demolished and re-built in the 1700s. This creates two very different architectural styles. The graves are in the churchyard. Some of the headstones are dated to the 1500s.

On the floor of the church nave, is a large tablet that lists all the vicars, or incumbents, from 1210 to 1965. There are forty-six in all. The church clock also serves as a carillon. It plays at 9am, 12 noon, 3 pm and 6 pm each day. Songs played are:
Sunday – We love the place, O God;
Monday – God moves in a mysterious way;
Tuesday – Life let us cherish;
Wednesday – At the name of Jesus;
Thursday – Bluebells of Scotland;
Friday – Sweet the moments;
Saturday – Home sweet home.

Print of St Michael's & All Angels Church before rebuild

There are eight bells that are tuned as follows, Treble and 2nd - 1870 recast 1910 by Taylor originally by Warner & Son, London; 3rd -1698 Henry Bagley of Chacombe for Thomas Cartwright; 4th -1649 HB (probably Bagley too) Inscription reads "Mary Cartwright gave this bell"; 5th – 1635 Inscription reads "God save our King"; 6th – 1620 Robert Atton of Buckingham, recast 1975 by Whitechapel Foundry, London; 7th – 1603, no additional information; 8th – 1617 Robert Atton of Buckingham, recast 1980 by Taylor. It weighs 16 cwt.

Most of the village houses were two up and two down, with a passage through the centre. A washhouse could be found behind the house. It was usually the place where the coal was also stored. Coal was used for heat and cooking. The outside lavatory was next to it. These looked like a toilet of today, but there wasn't a cistern for flushing. That was accomplished with a bucket of water, carried from the water butt by the back door.

All houses had back gardens. Some were much larger than others. Vegetables and flowers were grown for the house. The family pig was usually kept in the far corner of the garden, in its pigsty. The clothesline usually bordered the garden beds along the paths.

Other larger houses were usually designed for special needs, or because the family that lived there was of a higher standing in the village. These were usually farmers, tradesmen, artisans scholars, and the like. My mother's house, when we were young, was the two up two down kind, whereas my grandparent's was one of the others. In each house, the families added their own special touch, to make them feel like home.

Chapter 2
Aynhoe's One Room Schoolhouse

At one time the school was a two-room schoolhouse, but by 1944, with the limited number of children in the school, only one room was being used. It was the largest one. After the war there was an increase in children, and then the other room was opened up for the infants, four and five year olds. The teacher for that room was a Miss Gert. She wore her hair in two braids, that wrapped around her ears like pinwheels. She was also very religious and taught Sunday school.

At this time, in the village community, children started school the first day that it was open after their 4th birthday. So I started school February 14th 1944 my birthday being the 13th. My mother took me to the school, even though I knew the way. The teacher's name was Miss Govier, and she had taught my mother during her last year at the village school.

Painting by Julia Cartwright circa 1840
Aynhoe School big room

I do not remember much about the first morning, other than becoming aware of the surroundings, but the general feeling I had was that I liked it. I went home at 12 noon for dinner, and at that time I told my Mother that; school was fine, but I did not need to go back any more. She told me that wasn't the way it worked and that I was going to school from now on, everyday but weekends and holidays.

I had other ideas, so I was dragged kicking and screaming back to school in the afternoon. As the story goes, I screamed for three solid days, to the point that no one else could do any work. So Miss Govier sat me beside the piano, and had the other children stand around in a circle and sing.

'There was a little girl who had a little curl
Right in the middle of her forehead
When she was good she was very, very good
And when she was bad she was horrid.'

When I cried loud, they sang loud, and when I cried softly they sang softly.

Years later, I took our daughters to meet Miss Govier ,who was by then Mrs. Czeppe. She asked me if I remembered my first few days in school. I said "Oh yes. Very well". So did she; she said she never had another child like me, before or since.

The school was at the top of school lane. It was really in the middle of the village, just off of the Village Square. The school lane was between the Post Office and Off License, just up from Church House which was very large

and set back behind a very high wall. It always looked very grand to me. The church owned it; hence the name. At the top of the lane was the school playground. This had a very rough surface, with lots of loose, and not so loose stones, in and on it. Some were quite small like pebbles, but most were larger

Playground showing door in wall where Mrs. Oakey used to stand to watch the children play

about the size of teacups or mugs, and with very sharp edges. These were not at all comfortable on bare knees, when someone fell down.

To the right of the playground were storage sheds or garages, though no one had cars during this time of petrol rationing. There was a high wall facing the lane, with a door in it, that led to Oakey's house and their beautiful garden, full of colourful flowers. Mrs. Oakey lived there with one of her daughters, Ethel. Occasionally, Jack, one of her sons, lived there too. Sometimes when we were out to play, the older Mrs. Oakey used to open the door in the wall and watch us play. She was dressed in an old fashioned long black dress, with a high ruffle around her neck, that was edged with white lace. Her hair was white, and was pulled back into a bun at the base of her neck in the back. She never talked to us, but I thought she had a kindly face, and she seemed to love to watch us play. Apparently she was the widow of the Mr. Oakey, who was the village butcher when Gran was a little girl. The story goes, that he came to the village with a tin can that held all his worldly goods. He died a rich man, having owned the butchers shop, and one of the larger farms in the village. When I was about six, the old Mrs. Oakey died, and we were told we had to play quietly in the play-ground out of respect for her. Miss Govier thought it would be nice if all the children gave flowers for her grave. Miss Govier picked flowers from her garden, and arranged them in the shape of a large fan, and wrote on a card that they were from the village school children.

I decided that wasn't quite what I wanted, so I asked Gramp if I could pick a few flowers from his garden; he said I could. I picked only enough to make a very small fan of flowers, and tied them carefully with a ribbon. I wrote on a note that it was for Mrs. Oakey from Dawn Alsford. When school was over for the day, I took them up to the house, and gave them to her son, Jack. He thanked me so much. I felt good that I had done it. Imagine my disappointment when, after her funeral, I went to look at her grave and my flowers weren't there. I thought they must not have been good enough. I shed a few tears.

Later that day, Dad said he wanted to talk to me about something. He asked me if I had given flowers to Mrs. Oakey. I said I had, but they didn't like them because they didn't put them on her grave. He told me Mr. Oakey and the family were so touched by what I had done, that they decided to put them in her hands, on her chest, and they were buried with her. This way she would have them with her forever, and she loved flowers so much, that it was better than being on top of the grave, where they would die fairly quickly. Mr. Oakey just wanted me to know, and hoped it was all right with me. It was.

The school was built high enough to have been two stories, but instead the ceiling was just very

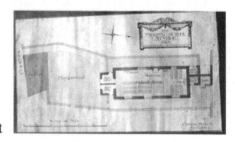

School plans 1830

24

high. There were two doors facing the playground, with windows above that looked like half circles, with points similar to those seen in churches. When there were lots of children going to the school, one door was for the boys, and one for the girls, with each leading into their own cloakrooms. From each cloakroom, doors led to the large school-room. It was oblong shaped, with the length running down from the doors. Each of the long walls had windows in them. The windows were very large, and let plenty of light in, but they were very high. So it would take an adult, standing on the window seat, to see out even the bottom of them. In the wall on the left were two large open fireplaces.

In the winter this was the only source of heat. Miss Govier used to keep them roaring, so we all stayed warm, and she ar-

Miss Govier with class circa late 1920's
Note the old combined desks, and high windows.

ranged our desks so we took full advantage of the heat they offered. Inside the fire screen she had metal benches, just the right height so that the top of them were directly in front of the hottest coals, like the ones that you'd use to make toast. On these benches, she would place our potatoes with our own special recognition marks on them. At 10am she would turn them all, so they would cook all the way through. Then at 11am, when we went out to play, she would give us each our potatoes to eat, wrapped in paper so we wouldn't burn ourselves, but they would keep our hands warm. I loved it if the skin on mine had been burned black. I can't remember any baked potatoes that ever tasted as good as those did.

At the far end of the classroom, there was a small house that looked like a log cabin. It was large enough to be a playhouse for children to function inside. My memory is not very clear about it, but there was furniture inside, and I seem to recall we could learn to do such things as; to set a table properly for a meal, wash dishes etc. If we put on plays for the school, it was done back in the same area. There was a door in the back wall, on the left into the second classroom, that wasn't used until after the war.

Miss Govier arranged the desks into small groups, and at different angles in the classroom. Each group had a different level of learning, but not necessarily a different year. She would conduct the teaching of a subject, then assign a project, and then move on to the next

Circa late 1920-30's Back of classroom showing log cabin

group. If a child progressed to the next level, then the child was moved up, and we didn't have to wait for the year to end to do that. We never went back because we wouldn't go forward unless we had completed that level.

The desks were the old type, that could sit two, and some would even seat six. The desktop was all in one piece. In other words, if you wanted to lift the top of your desk up, the whole thing went up. The same happened with the seat. Each section had an inkwell that a china type ink pot fitted in. We used what we called 'scratchy pens' with replaceable nibs. They were so called because of the scratchy sound they made as you wrote.

At Christmas time, all the desks were arranged in the more typical fashion of long rows, one behind the other. This was because we were all involved in getting things ready for Christmas. We made our own things for the Christmas show, plus all the decorations for the classroom. Because of the war, paper, glue and colouring utensils were unavailable. Paper from old exercise books, or anything else that could be reused, was cut into strips about two inches wide, and about 8-10 inches long. Then each one of these was coloured with whatever we had available. Sometimes we used crayons, sometimes watercolours. When these were all done, we made a paste with flour and water, so we could glue them together to make circles, that would be looped together to make chains. These would be hung across the ceiling to make it look very festive. Because of the size of the room, this usually took several days.

I remember one year there was a terrible accident. To put it in perspective, all the clothes we needed to purchase were rationed, and even then they were not that easy to come by. We all had one set each of Sunday best clothes, school clothes and play clothes. These were passed down to the next level, according to growth rather than wear, because most things could be mended to last a bit longer. Most Sunday clothes were bought at least two sizes too big to make them last. Occasionally something would happen, and we would have to wear something one day where it didn't belong; such as a Sunday outfit to school. We would be told how important it was to take great care of it.

Well, this particular day, one of the girls had to wear her Sunday best skirt. It was an especially pretty pink skirt that we all admired. It wasn't unusual for some of us to sit on the top of the desk behind us, when we were making the decorations, and have our feet on the seat. I guess it gave us more space to deal with the chains as they got longer. Well this girl did just that. She also had long pigtails (braids), and no-one noticed that the end of her pigtail went into the inkwell, and when she stood up, all the ink went across her pretty skirt and stained it something awful. She was so upset and so scared of what her mother would do, she was beside herself. Miss Govier just took her into the back room, and found a costume for her to put on. She then took the skirt, and spent the rest of the day working with it, until she was able to get the stain out. That type of ink is very difficult to get out, but she saved the day.

Miss Govier had a really great way of teaching. She would make it interesting, and show us short cuts to make things easier to understand, especially in maths. She taught one thing that has stood us all in good stead, and that is an easy way to count. It is especially useful for mental arithmetic. It works like this. Everything in counting is easier if one uses a pattern, or thinks of them as having partners. She would draw two boxes and give each a head two legs and two hands. The hands between the two boxes would be joined, making them partners. In the boxes would be numbers that when added together would add up to 10. For example: 7+3; 5+5; 6+4; 8+2; 9+1 or 3+7; 4+6; 2+8; 1+9. Once you have that in your head, it is easy to make up or see other patterns. One just breaks them back down to the original pattern, no matter where they are in the row. For example: 7+4+9+6+6+8= 40. With the first group you need 3 out of 4 to get the partner for the 7 leaving the 1 for the 9 to make its partner. Then you do the same with the next set 4 from the 6 for the other 6 that leaves the 2 for the 8. Once you get the matching partners together in your head, you can run through a list of numbers, adding them so rapidly that you don't have to hesitate a bit. It is a lot of fun just to see how fast one can do it.

I can honestly say, I don't know of any child who had Miss Govier as a teacher, that didn't love her. She was very strict, but very fair, and she could get things out of us that no other teacher I have had since could. I seemed to do fine in school, and I loved maths and reading. We were taught to read using the Beacon Readers, one to six, and by the time we were up to six they were normal stories. I got to level six by the time I was five. I couldn't get enough books to read. My writing was not so good, and even copying onto a page left much to be desired. I was told I had to slow my thoughts down, because my mind was going faster than my pen. I dealt with this problem all through my educational years and beyond, until one day, in my 40's, someone said to me you deal with your dyslexia very well. I never knew that was the problem, but after I thought about it, it all made sense. But mine was just in the writing of words and grammar, not reading or numbers. Again, I am getting ahead of myself.

My maths books were not a problem to write, and generally I had gold stars on my exercise pages, except for two pages that faced each other. On those 2 pages there were big red crosses, and 'LAZY' written in large red letters. For the laziness on the second page, I earned the punishment Miss Govier only dished out on very rare occasions. She would roll the sleeves up of the offending hand, place your palm down in her hand, and with her other hand give you several resounding slaps to the back of your hand. Your hand would become red, but I think it was our pride that was hurt the most. I can only remember getting this punishment once. Believe me there were no more lazy pages in my book.

Our School day started at 9am, our morning break was at 11am. Dinner was from 12 noon 'til 1pm, followed by an afternoon break which was at 3pm. School ended for the day at 4pm. We all went home for dinner, because we were all within walking distance of home, and it was normal to have our main meal at that time. Women tended, if they had families, to not go out of the village to work, and very few worked if they had young children. Meals would be prepared so they cooked whilst everyone was gone for the morning. Stews and the like were very common, as they were nutritious, and would cook without someone having to stand over the cooker. If my mother was doing the hairdressing, Gran used to cook the dinner for us all, and take care of us when we weren't in school.

After dinner, all the children would go up to Miss Goviers' house at number 4 to meet her, and then we would all walk to the school together. On these walks the topic of conversation could be quite varied.

Our school year went from about September 7th to around July 27th. We always had the month of August off. Teachers said it was too long a break but we didn't think so. The first official term of the year was from September 'til Christmas. We would be off until after the New Year when the second term started. That went until Easter, whether it was early or late. At the end of each term, there would be exams. We would have about ten days off for Easter, then the last term would go through until the end of July. At that time, the exams were to cover the work for the entire school year. We would have half term breaks, which would generally amount to a long weekend. There was one exception, and that was for the country children, when the half term break in the autumn was a week long. The reason for this was, that the potatoes had to be gathered in the fields. With the men away at war, there weren't enough people to get them in without the children helping. It was a fun time for all.

We were each assigned to different farmers, and would meet in their farmyards first thing in the morning. I was always assigned to Joe Watts' farm. He had a huge hay wagon, with panels that went out about a foot at the top rim. His big carthorse pulled it. Going to the fields, we all got to ride inside the wagon, along with the buckets we were going to use to gather the potatoes. When we got to the field, the women would take the buckets, and place them every so many feet. This was after the rows had been turned over, to expose the potatoes. Then we kids would go to a bucket, and start down the rows filling them as we went. When it was full, we just left it where it was, and went on to the next. The women would come along and pick up the full buckets, and take them back to the wagon, where Joe Watts and Derb Ayres would pile them inside it. We all kept working like this 'til lunchtime, then we would stop and have a picnic lunch in front of one of the hedge-rows. After we had finished eating, we would take off exploring, until the adults decided it was time to get back to work again.

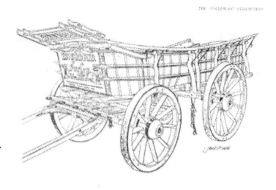

Type of Hay wagon Joe Watts used for hauling Children and potatoes

We would work 'til the wagon was as full as it could be, then we all piled on top of the potatoes for the ride home. The adults usually walked alongside. This went on all week, until all the potatoes were gathered and safe in the barns. The adults said the reason the children gathered the potatoes into the buckets, was because we were closer to the ground, so it wasn't backbreaking for us - this made perfect sense. One year, when my friends and I were older and knew how to ride our bikes, we got permission from our mothers to take our bikes to the fields, on the promise not to play around but to behave. Well, at lunchtime, Janet Watts, Cicely-Anne Abernathy and I, decided we were going to try and be cowboys, and ride the pigs in the large pigpen, just like we had seen in the movies. The pigs were in a very large yard, with roofing over half of it, and hayracks around the many posts holding the roof up.

The idea was; to climb onto the hayracks, and when a pig came by, drop down onto its back and ride it like a cowboy. All went well until the pigs got scared, and started charging all over the place to get us off their backs. Our laughing and whooping didn't help much. Finally the pigs ran into each other, and tossed us off their backs into the messiest part of the yard. By the time we got to our feet we were filthy. We knew we couldn't go back to the fields, or home, in this state. So we found an old water butt. The water in it was pretty green, but we thought it was the best we could do. We stripped to our knickers, and "washed" our clothes until they were not quite as bad as before, but much greener. They were wet of course, so we came up with the bright idea of tying them to the back of our bikes, and riding them up and down the road to dry them. By the time we had to go back to the fields they weren't quite as wet, but they were very ripe and no-one wanted to be anywhere near us. I am sure we all got a good hiding when we got home, but I don't remember that part of it.

Not long after the war ended, Miss Govier came to school with several large tins. She said they had been sent to the village by an American serviceman, who had really liked our village and the people in it. I think he came to the school and talked a few times. Maybe he was a teacher back in America. Anyway he had sent these tins that were full of cocoa, to be divided amongst all the villagers. It was his way of saying thank you!

The cocoa was divided so each child took a cupful home; this meant the larger families had more, because they had more to feed. For the households that had no children, according to the numbers in the house they were given a cup or more. So everyone got some. Now what was so special about this cocoa? Well if you had had to drink the cocoa we had during the war, you wouldn't ask! Ours was very dark and very bitter. It needed a ton of sugar to sweeten it, but we had little to no sugar to put in it, so it would be sweetened with golden syrup. Those of us that had not known anything else but our wartime cocoa, didn't know any better. That is until we got to taste this sent from America.

It was a light chocolate colour, and so sweet that it didn't need sugar in it. We were all very stringent with it, to try and make it last forever, because we didn't know if we would ever have anything like it again, in our lifetime. That was such a special gift. I just hope he knows how much we all enjoyed it, and what pleasure he had given the whole village.

Chapter 3
20 Station Road

20 Station Road, Aynhoe was my grandparents' home. We lived there until just before my sister June was born in 1942. Apparently my mother did not want to bring another baby into Gran and Gramp's house.

The reason for this was, that she did not want Gramp spoiling the new baby, the way he had spoiled me. We moved to 32 The Lane, Aynhoe. In all my subsequent memories this was our home while we lived in Aynhoe, and 'down home' was my grandparents' home. It is still called 'down home' by the family to this day.

20 Station Rd. Now 18 Round Town. Note the dark coloured wash house door entrance to the Rt of the house

The houses in our village are about 350-500 years old, built of stone, with walls three feet thick. Therefore all the windows have either window seats, or very wide window sills. These are great places for children to play or for the homeowner to keep their plants.

All the ceilings have exposed beams. Usually there was one large central support beam, that went the length of the room. Perpendicular to that, and about a foot apart, were the other beams going across the width of the ceiling. These were used to hang the hams, and slabs of bacon, that had been smoked or cured previously in the fireplace.

The fireplaces were very large open ones, that were used for cooking, and were the only source of heat for the whole house. There was an open grate about a foot wide, two and a half-feet high, and two feet deep, with 3 to 4 metal bars across the front, to hold the hot coals and cinders back. This was great for making toast, using a long handled toasting fork, so as not to burn your hand or scorch your shins, if you sat too close to it. To the side of the grate was the brick oven. To know what the temperature was for the cooking, it was necessary to put your hand on the metal door handle to gauge the heat.

Watching my grandfather do this, it seemed you could gauge how hot the oven was, by how quickly he removed his hand from the handle! My grandfather, called Gramp by all the grandchildren, would always check it for my Gran. If it was to be for pies, he would remove his hand pretty fast, and say "Just perfect for your pies David". My grandmother's name was Ada, but until just a few years before he died he always called her David. No one knows why.

About the time he started calling her Ada, he wrote this poem about her. He said he was watching her and it just popped into his head.

To My Ada
Do you remember my dear
A day long, long ago
A day when first we met
The sky was blue, just me and you
On the day when first we met

But long years have passed
Since then dear heart
And we have no regret
And I thank God for the day
When you came my way
On the day that first we met

Ada 1956

And now we are old and gray, dear
Sweet memory, we'll never forget
The sky is still blue
As it was for me and you
On the day that first we met.
G.E.P.

Now back to the house. Some of the fireplaces had a bread oven to the side, our house didn't have one, but my grandparent's did. The entire fireplace had big open tops, for cooking what is now cooked on

33

the top of a stove. Above this was the massive opening that went up the chimney. The chimney opening is where the hams would be hung to cure or smoke. When there wasn't a fire burning in the grate, one could lean over, look up the flue, and see the metal stakes in the walls. These were what the chimney sweep boys used to climb up, so that they could sweep it. This is how it was done in the nineteenth century. One could also see the large opening to the sky, which is why, when it rained and the fire was burning, we would hear "spits and spats", as the rain hit the fire and hot coals.

The upstairs, in most of these houses, were just two bedrooms, with the same window seats and beams in the ceiling as the downstairs. My grandparents house was larger than most. Gran said that at one time, many years ago, it was used to do some of the laundry for the Park House. That's why their washhouse was larger than in most of the homes, because other people needed to work at the laundry, in addition to those that lived there. Theirs was at the side of the house, and could be reached from the front through a separate door.

The washhouse was for doing the weekly wash. In there was a copper. It was a large copper bowl, built into a brick area, that had a grate in the bottom to light a fire to heat the water. The water would be heated to boiling, and then all the white clothes would be put in it to be boiled. This was to make them white. They used to say "Woe betide the woman that had dingy white clothes hanging on her line." After they had boiled them, the whites were taken out with a long stick - so as not to scald one with the boiling hot clothes - then put in one of the waiting tubs, to be washed and scrubbed on a scrub board. The clothes were then transferred to another tub to be rinsed. At each transfer from the tubs, the clothes had to be wrung out. Larger items were wrapped around their arms, as they worked down the entire length of the piece, wringing them out with their hands. After the rinsing they went into the blueing tub. This was usually placed under the mangle (wringer), so all you had to do was to pull it out and put it through the mangle. The art was to put it through the mangle folded, or at least in a way that caused the least amount of wrinkles, which saves on the ironing later.

With the coloured clothes, the process was less involved be-cause there was no boiling, and coloured clothes didn't need the blue-ing. All this sounds like a day's work; which of course it was. What I didn't mention was, that the day before all this took place - on a Monday - the water for the copper, and all the tubs, had to be carried from the village water pump. Our closest pump was about 300 yards away. It was only about 50 yards from my grandparents.

The fire under the copper heated the water for it, but the rest had to be heated on the grate in the main room - Summer and Winter. Monday was wash day and nothing else was done. Dinner was usually cold leftovers from Sunday, except of course for freshly cooked potatoes, or bubble and squeak (potatoes and cabbage fried in lard till golden brown) - excellent eating.

My grandparents mangle was something very special. It was huge, made of iron, very decorative, and taller than Gramp, he was 5'1". It had 2 large wooden rollers, about six inches thick. What made these roll were two large wheels at the side that worked on a cog mechanism. When I was down home on washday, I would help with the rolling. Gran would pass the clothes through from the front; Gramp would catch them at the back, and fold them ready to be hung up. My job was to work the wheels. They were so large, that when the handle got to the top, I couldn't reach it to bring it back down the other side. I would jump up on to the handle, and put my body weight on to it to bring it back down. Eventually, if I got enough rhythm to it, then I could be quite fast. But I imagine it took a lot of patience, on my grandparent's part, until that happened.

They always said I was such a great help to them, and they didn't know how they managed without me.

The washhouse had a separate doorway to the back garden, where the clothes were dried. There was another entrance, from the washhouse, into the interior of the main part of the house. This entrance had three steps going down, but the ceiling to the stairs was very low. Adults had to bend backwards, to prevent hitting their heads on the three-foot thick stone wall. There has not been an adult in the house, that at one time or another hasn't rushed to get to the main part of the house, and run headfirst into the wall. It sets you back on your heels in a hurry, and you forget whatever it was you were running to. As a child, I used to love to jump down two or three stairs at a time. On these stairs it would put your head so far down into your shoulders, that you felt like you were half your normal size, (or at least wished you

35

were). I did it more than once; I must have been a slow learner! When, as a family we reminisce, we always laugh about the washhouse steps with fond, though painful, memories.

On the main level was a small room known as the pantry, (it later became the kitchen). Off of this was a walk-in larder. One of the shelves was made of marble, because it stays cold, no matter what the outside temperature is. The perishables were kept on it, as refrigerators were unknown to us then. There was a door through the pantry to the hall, which was really just a passageway from the front door to the stairs door, and the rooms on either side of the passage. Under the stairs there was an area behind a door, where wood for kindling and burning was kept, and any vegetables that needed to be in the cool and dark. The doorway to the main room, had an army blanket hung on it, to keep the draughts out. It would balloon out into the living room. As children we loved to stand with our backs to it, and then just fall into it. If the draughts were really bad, it would hold us up for a brief second!

The main room was the living room, dining room and kitchen, all rolled into one. It was always cozy, and usually smelled of good things cooking. A large kettle was always just off the boil, in readiness to go to boiling point, if a pot of tea was needed. There was the large fireplace I have talked about earlier, with its high mantelpiece above, with nick-knacks on it. They looked like they had been there forever, and were too high to dust on a regular basis. To the left side of it, on the wall, is where Gramp kept his silver pocket watch. The town of Banbury presented him with this, when he and four others returned from the Boer War in Africa. This was just before he married my grandmother. It has an inscription on it, but with one mistake, they

Silver Pocket Watch

spelled his last name 'Parrish' with only one 'r'. The inscription read: Presented to Private G. Parish of the Volunteer Service Company. On his return from The War in South Africa 1901- by Inhabitants of Banbury & the Neighbourhood. On the back is the Oxford and Bucks emblem.

Every night before he went to bed, he wound his watch - just so many twists of the handle, then gently shake it side to side, look at it and hang it back up, I watched him do this so many times.

A year after he died, I found his watch just lying in a drawer. I asked Gran why it was there, thinking it would have been given to one of his sons. She said it didn't run anymore, that Denis (their youngest) had taken it to get it repaired, to be told it was beyond repair. It apparently hadn't run since Gramp went in the hospital, just before he died. Gran said it was meant to be. It had died with him. I couldn't believe it, so I wound it up, the same way I had watched him do it many times before, and it started right up. I said: "See its fine. They just didn't wind it correctly." Gran said: "It is yours, it was waiting for you to wind it, and you always were his favourite anyway." I told her I couldn't do that, it should go to one of his four sons, and that I could show whoever had it, how to wind it.

Several weeks later, when I was down home, Gran and Denis were there. Denis handed me the watch and said it was mine. I told them it wasn't right, it should go to one of the boys. Denis said they had checked with all of them. They all agreed it was rightfully mine, that Gramp would want it that way. It still runs to this day.

To the left of the fireplace was a cupboard, for all the dishes that were used for dining. Gramp always kept his Sharp's vanilla toffees in there, so that we could have one when we came to see them. He never ran out, which was incredible, because sweets were tightly rationed during the war, and for many years after.

In front of the fireplace were two chairs. Gran's on the right of the fireplace, with Gramp's exactly opposite on the left. Under the window, and behind Gramp's chair, was the velvet *chaise longue*. It had the large roll-back on the left, with the low back and carved wooden trim. I always thought it was so fancy, and it was comfortable, except for the horsehair that sometimes poked its way out, and scratched the back of our bare legs. Beside that, along the back wall, was the table. The top was natural wood, scrubbed clean. On this, all the work was done, and meals were taken. When it was not being used to work on, then a heavy, dark, fancy tablecloth covered it. When it was mealtime, a spotless white starched tablecloth was placed over the other cloth, to protect it. The table was always set at nighttime, ready for breakfast in the morning.

On the wall behind the table were pictures. Some were large photos in frames, and secured in these were all the grandchildren's pictures. They were never taken down, just added to. In the end the original picture in the frame was obscured.

To the other side of the doorway, was an oak chest of drawers that the downstairs linen was kept in. It was heavily carved and had fancy ornaments on top, along with the wireless (radio). To the right of the fireplace, above Gran's chair, was a wide shelf. On this Gran kept all her paperwork, such as bills and receipts. Her portable writing cabinet, that Gramp had made for her, was also kept there. It had a pull down lid that made into a mini writing table. In it she kept official papers, and some photos of the family when her children were young. But the best part was a drawer at the bottom. In there she had some old brooches, and some very old photos of her parents. One of them was her father sitting at his front door. He had a white beard, and behind him stood her mother, with her hair pulled back in a bun, neatly dressed in a long dark dress. They lived in the same village, but not the same house, that my grandparents lived in.

Between the chest of drawers and the corner, directly behind Gran's chair, was a very large painting of a battle scene. It was probably of the Crimean War. It had a very decorative gilt frame that was quite beautiful, but the picture was very sad. It showed a drummer boy about 12 years old, he was down on the ground apparently injured. Men were trying to help him up, with the battle raging all around them. I did not like the picture, but Gramp was always looking at it when he sat in his chair. It was directly in front of him, so it was hard not to look at it. Finally, one day, I asked him why he seemed to like the picture so much. His response was; "What picture?" I said: "That one you are always looking at it." He said: "Oh, that one. No I don't like it, it's an awful picture. I don't look at the picture, I just see what is going on outside. Come and see." When I sat in his chair and looked at it, I couldn't see the picture, but it was the perfect size to give a full reflection of the window behind him. The glass covered the picture so he could see what was happening outside. Because Gran sat with it behind her, she didn't see it either!

There was a door at the bottom of the stairs, and it had two purposes. Firstly it kept the draft from coming down, secondly it separated downstairs from upstairs. The stairs wound around very tightly to the next floor. Once, when I was very young, Mum and Gramp were arguing about something, and Gramp opened the stairs door, went up two stairs, turned and continued arguing. I thought that was a clever thing to do, as Gramp was five foot one, and Mum was five-foot eleven inches tall! Gramp wrote a poem about Mum when she was young; she says she never liked it.

FAIR NORAH

I know of two bright eyes
That are smiling
They belong to a maid tall and fair
They smile like the rain sun
Through the raindrops
And drive away all sorrow and care
And the name of that fair maid
Is Norah
She is all the world to me
I would give much on the morrow
Those two smiling eyes to see

Oh Norah, fair Norah
The brown bird is singing
High on the tree top just over the way
Oh Norah, fair Norah, the sun is shining
Outside the old cottage where you
Used to play

Norah 1938

Oh Norah, fair Norah
The night it has fallen
The stars in the heavens
Are shining so bright
But where ever you may be
My thoughts will be with you
Tall Norah, fair Norah
God bless you goodnight.
G.E.P.

On the next floor, was where their house was very different from others in the village. There was a small landing, and to the left was a door to a small room, that was sometimes a bedroom, and sometimes a salon for hairdressing. Most of my grandparent's children were hairdressers. In front of the stairs was a door to Gran and Gramp's bedroom. Years ago, when the house was a laundry for the squire, this room was the living room for the family of the house. It was larger than most English bedrooms of the time, and had a small fireplace and beams across the ceiling. As Gran and Gramp's bedroom, it was a great place for a little girl to explore, or listen to stories about years before. Especially if she had an insatiable curiosity, as I did.

The main object in the bedroom, was the large iron bedstead. The head and footboard were mostly black, with gold trim and cream coloured ceramic trim balls at the corners. The frame, and the metal springs that held the mattresses, were about a foot and a half above the floor. The first mattress was about 6" thick and made of straw. It was heavy and rarely, if ever, turned. The next was a hard flock filled mattress, about 4" thick, also not turned often, and next was a softer flock mattress, that was turned once a week, again 4" thick. Then, the best of all, a thick feather mattress, that had to be shaken up and turned daily. It was then gently made level, by spreading your fingers widely apart, and working from the centre out, with a movement similar to a piano player pounding the keyboards. When it was as level as possible, then the sheets and blankets covered it. The pillows were placed gently at the top, then the counterpane and eiderdown decorated it. All had to be done carefully, so as not to disturb the feathers.

When I slept ' down home' they used to make a bed up for me on the floor. Because of the height of their bed off of the floor, I could see under it. When Gramp went downstairs to do his chores, to get the house ready for Gran, as he passed me he would say: "Go on my duck. Go and get in my hole." I'd climb out of my bed and get into Gramp's 'hole' in the bed and snuggle up to Gran. It was always so warm and cozy. The hole was the indent that his body had made in the feather mattress, during his night's sleep.

At six o'clock, Gramp would bring Gran and me a cup of tea in bed, to help us to wake up, and to tell us what the day was like outside. He was an expert weather forecaster. I have never been a lover of tea, but I always drank Gramp's without a complaint. After he had allowed enough time for us to drink the tea and wake up, he would bring a large jug of hot water up for us to wash up with. He would always say there was enough for the both of us, and to be very careful because it was very hot.

Gran would thank him, and get the water. While she did that, I would climb over the 'hump' that had formed in the mattress between them and snuggle into Gran's 'hole'. Her hole was even softer and cozier than Gramp's was. I would lie on my side and watch her washing up at her wash stand. This was when I used to hear so many stories. I will tell you more about those 'Gran's stories' later. They would be triggered by something in the room, or something that 'just crossed her mind', or one of the many unending questions I had.

The washstand was on the left, just inside the bedroom door. My bed was next to it on the floor, where her dresser would be when I wasn't there. Her washstand was bigger than any other I have ever seen, before or since. It was about two feet deep and four feet wide. It had a splashboard around the sides and back. The top had holes in it for certain items, like the wash basin, round soap dishes etc. Gran's basin set was very complete; it was dark orange in colour at the outer edges, gradually getting paler as it went into the centre where it was cream in colour. There was the large wash basin with a large jug in it with the cold water, to cool down the hot water Gramp gave her. There were two round soap dishes with lids, a long oblong dish without a lid, two upright pots with lids; they looked like Chinese ornamental ginger pots. Gran said they were designed to put toothbrushes in, but that they weren't very convenient. She had snow white starched linen lace-edged mats on the top, to catch the drips, and a folded loose linen towel to wipe the side of the jugs.

The lower shelf was level without holes in it. This had a plain linen cloth across the entire surface. On this she kept the 'his and hers' 'Gerries' (chamber pots), and the slop bucket. This had a lid with a raised knob that had open areas through it, I presume to let the fumes out. It also had a large straw wrapped carrying handle. This bucket would be carried up to the lavatory each morning, and emptied, washed out and disinfected. Under this shelf was a drawer that went the width of the cabinet. In there, Gran kept her bathroom supplies.

If I wasn't sleeping there, the wall that formed the front of the house, was where Gran's dresser stayed. Hers was a chest of drawers, painted medium blue, with a mirror stand on top, that had two very small drawers in the base. It had a very shiny surface. There were up-right arms that held the mirror, so that it could swing back and forth, according to how you needed it to look at yourself. The little drawers were where Gran kept all her best jewellery, such as her opal engage-ment ring, and cameo brooch. There were a lot more than those two pieces, but jewellery has never impressed me much. My sister June used to love going through Gran's "juuwelry" drawer, as she called it, so she probably knows all that was in it.

Beside her dresser on the wall was a photo of Gran in a heavily carved frame. It was taken in 1899 when she was 17 years old. It was just her head and shoulders, and showed a dress that had a high collar around her neck, with a white lacy frill. The bodice looked like it had many tucks in it, all edged with satin ribbon, along with a wide frilly yoke, also edged with satin. Pinned on the left side of the inside of the yoke were two roses. One could be seen easily, and the other was a little harder to see. Gran said she had made the dress by hand, because she didn't have a sew-ing machine at the time. The dress was medium blue with darker blue sat-in trim. It had a full skirt with a long frill on the bottom, which would drag  along the ground, so she would have to hold it up to prevent it from get-ting dirty. The roses were yellow and dark red, taken from the garden where she lived and worked at that time. She said, many years later, that the dress was still fine, so she wore it to get married in.

Next to the dresser was the window with the window seat, and in the corner on the other wall was a cupboard. In the top section were things like old hat boxes, and other treasures. One of the hatboxes had Gramp's bowler hat, and some of Gran's big fancy hats with huge hat-pins. My sister liked to dress up in these, and put on a fancy dress parade for Gran. I always thought that was funny, because I couldn't imagine Gramp in a bowler, and June thought Gran's hatpins looked like she would stick them in her head. Gran said you don't notice them hurting when you get older, and Gramp always wore the bowler when he went to London. She said he looked quite dapper when he was dressed up in his city finery.

Next to the cupboard was the fireplace. It was just a little one designed to sit around, not to cook on. Then there was a blank wall, where Gramp's chest of drawers was located. Next to it was another cupboard just like the first one, mostly used for blanket storage. Then came the wall with the bed, and two bedside tables, also made by Gramp. These also had snow white lacy cloths on them. There was a large patterned rug that nearly covered the entire floor.

To the left of the stairs was another set of stairs, that went up to the two attic bedrooms. Each of these rooms was large enough to hold a double bed, a chest of drawers and a wardrobe. The window between these two rooms was at floor level, about two feet high. A section of the wall had been taken out, so that both rooms could benefit from the light.

There is a story told about this window: At the start of the war, if the people that were living in and around London, had families they could stay with in the country, they were told to move there. They called it being evacuated. Consequently, all of Gran and Gramp's son's wives were sent to live with them, and of course my mother - who was their only daughter - was there as well. At first it was very cramped, but eventually each found a place of their own to live, that was away from London and as a result safer.

As the story goes, I was a toddler, Mum was very pregnant with my sister June, and Mum and Gran were making the bed in the first attic room. Mum had her back to the window, when Gran silently signaled for her to look at the window. The window was open, and I was standing upright on the windowsill, with my toes hanging over the edge of the sill. Mum said she knew if they called to me, I would step forward before I turned round, and then fall two stories to the stone pavement. So Mum lay down quietly on her large tummy, and gradually crawled to where I was. She said; praying all the time I wouldn't move before she got there. She made it, and when she got within reach, gently put her arm around me and pulled me towards her. Then she and Gran cried with relief. Of note, it obviously had no effect on me, as I have never been afraid of heights, although I have always been cautious of that window, whenever little ones have been around. I believe this story being recounted taught me that.

Gramp's pride and joy was his garden behind the house. There was really no garden in the front, because the front door opened onto the path beside the road. But, as is typical in England, if there is any possible space to put a plant, you'll find it. So in front of the house, under each window, is a garden about a foot in depth. Under the living room window was a privet hedge, and beneath that would be spring bulbs, wallflowers, and summer annuals. Under the other window would be the same flowers, but, instead of the hedge, there was the apricot tree, that fanned out across the wall of the house. Years later they had two wooden tubs, that I had made for them for their Golden Wedding Anniversary. In those they put geraniums, alyssum and lobelia.

Gramp's back garden was a combination of flowers, shrubs, vegetables and fruit. The garden was level with the upstairs in the back, so it was necessary to go up the steps, to get into the garden through the washhouse. At the top of the steps, on the right, was a flowerbed with climbing roses over the fence, to separate them from the neighbour's garden. In the flowerbed I remember; lilies of the valley, violets, spring bulbs and mint, (looking back, with what I know now, I don't know how the mint didn't invade everything). There always seemed to be something blooming in this flowerbed. This bed, and the one to the left, was raised with small stone walls to keep the soil back.

Gramp & Denis in garden 1928

The bed on the left was the main part of the garden. The front of it, closest to the path always had flowers. Ones I remember specifically were; Canterbury bells, snapdragons, rose bushes and standard roses. One of the standard roses he really liked, he called it a cabbage rose, because, when it opened, it looked like a cabbage. Behind these was a row of gooseberry bushes. He showed us how to get the first and sweetest ones each year. To do this you had to sit under the bush, or as close as you could to get under it, and then reach under and pick the softest and ripest from there.

Behind these were his vegetables, all in neat rows. He would tell us the best time to harvest the different ones. One thing in particular I remember, was never harvest the Brussels sprouts until after a frost had been on them. That will make them crisper and sweeter. He showed me how to braid the shallots after they had dried, so they could be hung up for storage. Those would be the extras, that Gran didn't need for making pickled onions. Down the sides, and across the back, was planted a narrow row of flowers.

Narrow paths ran on either side of this garden, and across the back. The other side of these paths, on the left and across the back, there was another narrow flowerbed. But on the other side was Gramp's special interest. His strawberry patch! Every year he would take us up, so we could see how the strawberries were progressing. Then the great day would arrive. June and I would go up and watch Gramp pick the first one of the season, and it was always the largest too. After he picked it, we would ceremoniously follow him into the house. He would go to the cupboard, and take out an eggcup and a tea-cup, putting them both on the table, then summon Gran to come and watch. First he would put the strawberry into the eggcup, showing the strawberry was bigger than an egg. Then he would put it in the teacup. This would usually show that it wouldn't even fit in a teacup. We would all admire it, and then he would take it out, cut it in half giving it to June and me to eat. I have never eaten a strawberry yet that was as good as Gramp's first strawberry of the year.

We would always hear how the garden was coming along, what was in bud, and how long 'til they would be blooming. I remember one year Gramp thought his tulips were going to give 'a real show'. We were all in the living room, when June came in with her hands full of something. She went up to Gramp and said, "Look pretty, smells nice." Her hands were full of tight tulip buds. Gramp looked down and said "My poor bloody tulips!" We all went up to the garden, to see if there were any buds left on the plants - unfortunately there wasn't one!

The final important area of the garden, was behind the ten-foot high wall where the strawberries grew. It was known as 'the long walk'. It went the entire length of the garden, and at the end of it was their toilet, not at all convenient to the house. I thought that 'the long walk' was the name for toilets.

Years later, after we had moved to Oxford, and my first day in a city school, I held up my hand to be excused to go up 'the long walk'. No- one understood what I was talking about. I guess eventually they figured it out, but what I remember next, was everyone laughing at me. The teacher said that it was because I was a country girl, and not a city girl. She said it as though it made me less than them.

From that day on I never liked her, and I vowed I would never ever be a city girl. I would never like the city, and in fact I decided I was better than they were, because I did come from the country. As months went by, that same teacher, a Miss Partridge, continued to ridicule the country people. The final straw came when she said country people didn't know how to garden. They didn't plant anything in any order, but mixed all the plants and colours up, all 'higgledy, piggledy'. I had finally had enough! I stood up and told her, and the whole class, that I thought country people were better than city people, and country people knew how to plant better gardens than any city person did, because they planted gardens naturally, like God meant them to be! That, my Grandmother had a saying: "Soldiers stand in lines, flowers don't!"

Chapter 4
Two Up and Two Down - 32 The Lane

This was the home that my mother, June, and I moved into after June was born. 32 The Lane or 32 Aynhoe. Either one was our address, because at that time the numbers were not repeated in the village. It made life much easier. Years later an outsider came in, with 'know it all ideas', named the streets officially, and numbered within the streets. We had perfectly good names for the streets before they were changed. But, as is typical with outsiders, they always think they know better than the families that have been there for generations. Outsiders wonder why they are so unpopular. It wouldn't take too much to ask the locals before they take over.

Norah Parrish 1919

I digress: Mum - Norah Eileen Parrish - was born in the house known as 'down home', on 19th July 1918, the fifth child, and only daughter. My father, Sydney Melbourne Matthew Alsford, was away at war, so he was only there very briefly. This was usually before he went back to the front, after recovering from his latest injury. Dad was born in Portsmouth,

Sydney Alsford 1916

Hampshire on 10th November 1914 - the eleventh, and youngest child, to Samuel and Agnes (Grubb) Alsford. He was named Sydney Melbourne, because, the story goes, that by the 11th child Grandma had run out of names. So he got that name, because Grandpa was half way between those Australian cities when he was born. Grandpa retired as a Warrant Officer from the navy, after 23 years of service.

Mum said I was a miserable baby, and cried constantly. This one particular night, while we were still living 'down home', I was especially bad and would not stop crying. She had been walking the floor with me for hours. She had the lights off, so she could have the blackout curtains up. She stopped to look out the window, when the thought crossed her mind to throw me out. She was so scared of her thoughts, that she threw me across the room onto her bed to get me away from her. When I hit the bed, I bounced several times, gave two or three quick gasps and stopped crying. That was it, I never cried again at night! Mum often said; that if she had known that was all it took, she would have done it a lot sooner!

My sister, June Noreen Alsford was born in an Oxford hospital in 1942. From that time on, Mum moved her hairdressing business to the room at the top of the stairs at number 32, and Gran came to our house each day, to take care of us while Mum worked.

June Alsford 1942

Number 32 was a very small house. It was attached to another house, of the exact same size, and both shared the same walled back garden. The walls to the garden were very high, almost level with the bottom of the roof on the house. In the back garden, each had its own washhouse, with the usual built in copper, and a place to store the coal and wood for burning in the fireplace. Next to that was the toilet. Outside each back door was the essential water butt. This water was used for flushing the toilet and washing our hair, because it was soft water, and accordingly will make ones hair shine. Inside it was the same as Gran's, as far as the beams and the thickness of the walls go. But the fireplace for cooking etc. was much smaller. That did not stop Mum from cooking some great meals on it though.

There was a centre passageway, that went from the front door straight through to the back door. The floor in the passageway was made of natural flagstones. They were very uneven, with lots of dips in them, where water would settle when washing the floor. To the right was a door through to the pantry. In there was the table to do the kitchen type work. There was a larder for the food and cooking utensils, plus a bench to keep the buckets of water, for both home use and hairdressing. Water was constantly on the fire for hairdressing. Most of the women came to Mum after they had washed their hair, then Mum just had to wet it down before she did what they wanted.

Next to the pantry door, was the door to under the stairs, and then the door that led upstairs. On the left side of the passageway was the opening into the living room, with the usual army blanket hanging across it to keep the draughts out. There was only one cupboard in this room, to the left of the fireplace, and in there Mum kept all her dishes. She had easy chairs on either side of the fireplace, with a dining table opposite it with chairs around. The room was much smaller than Gran's, so furnishings had to be smaller. After the war, Dad made a drop-leaf table, to give even more space in the room. It was designed so that, when the leaf was down it looked like a tall cupboard, with cabinets in the top. The large flat piece at the bottom, became a large table top when lifted up.

In this room is where we all had our weekly baths. We used one of the galvanized wash tubs. It wasn't very long but it was deep. Saturday was bath night, and of course the water had to be carried from the pump, or if the rain butt was full, that was used and heated up on the fire. We had to have extra water heating, so that when one got out of the tub, more was added to make it hotter. The way it worked was, that once in three weeks you got the clean water, and the following two weeks you were either second or third getting in. It has to be done this way, when you don't have hot running water in the house. The rest of the week, in the mornings, we had stripped washes at the basin.

At the top of the stairs there was a small room, with a window in it. This was where Mum did the hairdressing, until close to the end of the war. It then became mine and June's bedroom, and Mum moved her hairdressing back to the small room down home.

I remember the night the planes were flying over for D-Day. Lying in bed, with the lights off and the blackouts up, I watched them. The sky was black with them, and I could hear people going past under our window saying: "This is it; it has got to be it." There was a lot of anxiety in their voices, so I knew this must be something really important. The planes seemed to keep going for hours. I remember having the sensation of butterflies in my stomach, but I am not sure I fully realized why.

In the past, I had spent many hours listening to planes coming back from bombing raids over Germany. Almost every night, there would be at least one that would sound like it had been damaged, and was just limping back home. They would go 'round and round' up in the sky. Mum said it was to use up what fuel they had left on board, to make it safer for them if they had to crash land. The sound the plane made was awful. You'd feel they are never going to make it, and just pray that they would come down safely. It never crossed my mind they could come down on us! It was just the worry for their safety. It is not a sound I ever want to hear again. I am happy to say, I do not ever remember hearing one of them crash.

Next to the small room was the large bedroom, that after the war was my parent's room. It is also the room my brother was born in, on 17th May 1945, and named Norman Melbourne Alsford. He was born with German measles, which the doctor said was very rare. Neither my sister nor I caught it from him.

Norman & Syd Alsford 1946

When I was about 3 years old, at Christmas time, Mum took me to Northampton to a pantomime. We probably went with a coach tour, because like everyone else we didn't have a car, and Mum didn't drive anyway. Pantomimes are popular to this day at Christmas time. They vary greatly in subject matter. Some popular ones are Cinderella, Dick Whittington, Jack and the Beanstalk, and Aladdin. In Pantomime, a woman always plays the leading man. She is usually tall and slim; wearing bright coloured clothes, that include tights and short tunic type suits.

The one we went to see was Aladdin. I remember being quite happy with it all, until the wicked wizard locked Aladdin in the cave. The way it was done on stage, you could see Aladdin in the cage, and then there was a floor above with the wizard standing on it. Aladdin was acting really scared. That was enough for me, I started shouting and screaming for the wizard to let him out, and as usual I wouldn't stop. Mum said the audience was laughing at first, and then they seemed to get concerned for me. In the end the wizard came to the front of the stage, and said loudly, to be heard over my screams: "Little girl if you will wait a little while, I will let Aladdin out of the cave. He won't be hurt." I eventually calmed down and the performance went on. To this day I can clearly see that stage scene and the wizard coming forward to say something to me. I did not remember what he actually said, but my mother told me.

Hairdressing in the forties was very complicated, and some of the things they used smelled awful and made your eyes burn. The perms were the worse. There was this huge machine which, after their hair had been rolled up into roller type gadgets, were pushed into tubes, that were attached to wires, that went into the top of this machine. After it had been hooked up for a while, it had either smoke or steam coming up from it. All the lotions or chemicals they used, were very strong smelling. It seemed to take hours to do a perm. There were scissor shaped tongs that were heated, and the hair rolled into them. It made very small waves. I think they were called Marcel waves. I used to sit at the top of the stairs, and watch 'til the smells got too bad, then I'd leave.

For as long as I can remember, my sister June has been very artistic and a real comedian. Even when she was very young she would imitate accents, expressions and movements of people. She would do it to the extent that you would beg her to stop, because your jaw and sides would ache so much from laughing. With age and practice, she has refined this skill to an art. She has the personality to be the life and soul of any gathering, large or small. She can remember jokes and stories from years ago, and embellish on them at will. As a child, she would constantly make up rhymes about people in the village, along with help and encouragement of her closest friend Suzanne Parrish. At that time Suzanne was no relation, but is now a cousin by the marriage of her mother to our Uncle Denis. Some of the rhymes they would just keep to themselves, and giggle about it, while June walked behind the person imitating their walk, movement or expressions. All at a safe distance not to get caught.

One she would imitate was a Mr. Stayton. He had a considerable limp, and June said he had a peg leg. I don't know if that was true. When he walked, the limp was very pronounced, and at the same time he would whistle just one constant note, without seeming to take a breath. June got the walk and whistle off pat. When she was imitating someone, it was very important not to be in front of the person she was imitating, because it was impossible not to laugh. Then the person would turn to see what we were laughing about. June could stop instantly, have a straight face and say something very nice to the person. This made us laugh even worse. Then they'd get angry with us, because they thought we were laughing at them, when in reality we were laughing at June. She got us into more trouble with her antics. They were so spontaneous, you could not avoid them, and there was never any instigation. She didn't need any!

There was one person in the village, Molly Berry; who did not get off that lucky. To some degree she asked for problems. She was the one in the village, as is common in all communities, that always harassed the kids. She lived next door to my grandparents, and her father lived up in the Alms Houses. He was really nice and a kindly old gentleman, but his daughter did not inherit any of those qualities. When we walked past her place, or played on the path in front of 'down home', she would come out, shake her fist at us, and tell us to get away from her house. No amount of reasoning made her change her attitude. So June and Suzanne made up a rhyme. It was a really terrible rhyme, and they would sing it outside her door, along with wild expressions. They would keep it up until she came out and threw a bucket of water on them. That would set them off even worse, until Gran would come out and put a stop to it.

Gramp had appropriate nicknames for June. When she was being mischievous it was ''Arriet and when she was being mean or unkind 'Spitfire'. They fit her well. His nickname for Norman was Matty. He didn't have one for me.

Chapter 5
Village Life and the Villagers

I will begin with what the village, and the village life, was like in 1940, starting with shortly after I was born. Also additional information from earlier times. This as has been told to me by older family members, and other villagers.

The population of Aynhoe, during the war years, was probably around 900 - not counting the military people that were billeted there. The houses are all built of stone and, of course, there are a lot of dry stone walls everywhere.

During the war the village had three greens; one at the top of the village, another at the bottom, and a third at the top of Station Road, where the village stocks are located.

In addition to the stores, located in the village square, there were the delivery people. Each

Walt Parrish in stocks 1932

had a van designed and fitted out, according to the needs to show off their wares. The baker, fishmonger, butcher and greengrocer came around twice a

week. Others would come around weekly, such as the coal merchant and the man that sold shoes. Still others would come around monthly, such as the organ grinder to sharpen knives etc. and the dry goods person. My favourite was the tinker. He had a tall square van, with all kinds of goods hanging on the outside, that rattled and jingled as he went along the road. You could enter his van

Hoods of Banbury Tinker's Lorry

from the back. The passage through it was very narrow, and the shelves went up to the top. I couldn't see much beyond the first 3-4 feet up, but all the shelves were stocked to capacity. All the vendors used to like to chat about what was going on in the next village, and around the county, while they waited on you at the same time.

There was another kind of delivery we used to get at that time, but it was erratic. It was when the Gypsies came around. They were true Gypsies – the Romanies. The women dressed in colourful blouses, and skirts of bright colours, with lots of embroidery on them. Their skin was darker than ours, and their hair was jet black. Even the older women didn't seem to have grey hair. They would go door to door, with their baskets full of wares for sale – brightly coloured ribbons and clothes pegs to sell. They would offer to tell you your fortune. We were told never to have the door wide open when talking to them. That way they couldn't see what you have inside. It was wise to buy a little something from them if you possibly could, so they wouldn't come and rob you to get even. The most important thing we were told, was to stay away from their camp, because they; "stole little children".

They always had their camp at the top of First Crossing, in the spinney. They would have their very decorative Gypsy caravans in a half circle, and a fire burning on the ground in the middle. The horses, that pulled the caravans, were tied up close to the trees. They looked so interesting and quite harmless to us, but we thought we wouldn't risk it, and would stay hidden so they couldn't see us. I remember one year, after all the Gypsies had moved on, we went up to where their camp had been, to see if they left anything interesting behind. They had - they had left one caravan, a horse, and a very old man. We were within his vision before we noticed it, and he called us to come and talk to him.

We asked him why he hadn't gone with the others. He said he had been taken poorly, and was going to wait a few days before moving on, to catch up with the others. We asked him about all the pretty painted decorations, and designs he had, on the outside of the caravan. He said each one was done to the owner's liking. He asked us if we would like to see inside. We didn't hesitate, as by this time we felt perfectly safe with him. Inside, the woodwork was beautifully carved and shiny. The cloth coverings were mostly red with patterns on them, as were the curtains. There was no extra space inside, but there were so many built-ins and a set place for everything. He said when you lived like this you had to be tidy, and put everything up when you were finished with it.

He told us the sofas made into beds. We were all very impressed, and really didn't want to leave. He gave no hint at all of wanting to steal us. I don't know about the other kids with me, but I never told my mother about it.

When my mother was a small child, there was a Romany Gypsy lady, called Mrs. Cotey Smith. She came to the village each year with her family, and stayed longer than the others. She was well liked and respected by all the villagers.

Aynhoe Potato Race 1930's

She is the lady in the picture with her hands on her hips. She was known to be hard working and honest. My mother remembers her for her fantastic cooking skills. When the family was in the village, Mrs. Cotey Smith would ask my grandmother if my mother, Norah, could play with her daughter Helen, who was about the same age. Mum said she would spend the whole day with her. Mrs. Cotey Smith cooked their whole dinner outside on the open fire, including a cake. It was all delicious, especially the cake, and she always served large slices! Helen later married well, and was kind and considerate to the people she had known as a child; just like her mother had been.

The churchyard was another place, that as children we definitely did not want to be after dark. There are some that the grave stones appear solid, in as much they have four sides, and a top like a table or a chest. I used to think these were the tables where, after dark, all the dead people came out of their graves and ate their meals. There were a lot of them, because there were a lot of dead people there. That is why I was never going to be caught in the churchyard after dark. It was my job, on Saturdays, to go and clip my Great Grandparents Wrighton's graves. All we had was the single hand scissors type clippers, that I had to use two hands on, because my hands were too small to do it otherwise.

Typical of all children, I would be busy playing, and would keep putting it off until it was getting dark. Mum would say: "Dawn. Do you want to cut those graves in the dark?" They had to be clipped ready for

Sunday. I would run around there so fast, clip at top speed, and run back out even faster, so the dead people wouldn't be out before I left. The gate from the church always creaked, and the Yew trees whined with the slightest breeze, which always gave me the additional spurt to get out of there. I think it was this practice each week, that later gave me the capabilities I had, of winning so many 100 yard dashes in our school track tournaments!

Our village pub was the Cartwright Arms. After going through the gate, there is an open way to behind the pub, that led to Joe Watts' other barn, milking shed and more of his pigsties. Janet Watts and I used to go down to Common field, after school each day, to bring his cows up for the evening milking. During the day, his cows were kept in the field on Common Hill. This is where the wild cowslips grew prolifically. These are the same type cowslips that Peter Rabbit made into wine, from the stories by Beatrix Potter.

Coming back was all uphill, so the cows, like us, were in no great hurry. There really wasn't much to it. The cows, numbering ten to twelve, ambled along in front of us, and we walked along behind with a long stick, so we could pat them on their rumps if they got too interested in the hedgerows. They are great for wild blackberries, flowers, birds' nests or anything else that stimulated ones curiosity, to slow the journey down, whether you were a child or a cow. Some of the hedgerows are hundreds of years old.

My great-grandfather, Edwin Wrighton, being a master hedger, worked many of these hedgerows in his time. My grandmother said hedgers are very proud of their work, and that it took a lot of skill to maintain them correctly. It is very dangerous work, because their tools are so sharp it is very easy for them to cut themselves. Losing fingers or eyes is one of the

Joe Watts barn yard behind the Cartwright Arms 1940's

big hazards. He was unusual for that day and time because he could both read and write.

56

Now back to the cows. We would walk them through the village, up to the Cartwright Arms, open the large gates if they weren't already open, and go through to the milking shed, where Joe Watts and Derb Ayres would milk them. When we got them to the milking shed, we helped to wash them down. After that we were free to play around the yard.

If they needed any mangolds ground up for the cows, or cow cakes for feed, then we would get those for them. Otherwise we just played. We would play either up in the loft of the barn, or by walking along the walls of the back end of the Cartwright Arms by the pigsties. At the end of these, there was usually a small hayrick that we used to like to jump on to. It was a nice soft landing. I remember once my mother caught us doing it, and told us it was too dangerous, because Joe & Derb were not too careful about leaving scythes in the hayrick, and they could cut our legs off. We continued doing it, but we did check for scythes before we did any jumping.

After the cows had been milked, Joe would take them up to the Big Butts for the night. This was one of his fields, that was only about 50 yards from his milking shed, so it was a quick trip for the early morning milking time. After the morning milking, one of them would take the cows down to Common Hill field for the day, and the two of them would take the milk in large buckets, down to the farmhouse to run through the cooler. The way they carried them was, with a wooden yoke that rested on their shoulders, and the buckets were hooked to them at arms' length, so they could hold them steady with their hands. This way they were able to carry much larger buckets, because the shoulders were taking most of the weight.

When we were kids, the Big Butts was used for sports events such as football and cricket. I remember one time, when the village boys wanted to have some different competition for a football game, it was arranged to have some of the German POW's to be brought to the village, to play against them. Now remember, we understood Germans were Gerries that dropped bombs on us. 'Gerries' were also what we called the chamber pot that went under the bed, that we used to relieve ourselves during the night. So there was a big discussion, between all the children, as to what these Gerries would look like! We didn't think they would look like what went under our bed, but we thought that maybe their heads would be shaped kind of like them.

The day arrived, and we all decided we would stay hidden behind the big Elm trees that went around the field, but fairly close to the changing hut, so we could get a good safe view of them. Our village boys didn't have kit, mostly because of cost and rationing, so they looked a rag-tail bunch, but they were good players. The Gerries got off the bus and they had kit. Their shirts and shorts were bright orange, and looked very smart. But most of all they looked just like everyone else. Some tall, some short, all about medium build with normal shaped heads! In fact one in particular sticks in my memory to this day. He was fairly tall, and had black straight hair parted on the side. He had a very nice face ,and a friendly smile when he looked towards us. We all decided they looked like us, so it was ok to come out from behind the trees and watch the game.

I have no idea of the results, or if there were more games. There probably were. After the war a lot of the POWs stayed on. They had made friends over here, and apparently there was nothing for them to go back to in Germany. Maybe their families had all been killed. There were a lot of families wiped out on both sides during the war. As we were told; it is to be expected. It is a fact of life when there is a war going on. Gramp had a saying about the Germans and the French that went like this – "You could always trust a German, because you knew when he was your enemy. But you could never trust a Frenchman, because you never knew which side of the fence he was on."

There was another field close to the village. It was on the northwest side, on the opposite side of the Brackley Road from the houses, and it was called Wensdon. According to Gran this was an old Saxon name. There were no longer any houses in it, but over a hundred years ago there was a home and bakery. One of our Wrighton ancestors apparently lived there, and she was considered a good baker, according to the archives about the family. This field sloped down the hill, and at the bottom of it was where the open septic tanks were for the village. I don't know why but they never smelled. In fact we would walk around the concrete edges of it, without a thought that we could fall in. Beyond the septic tanks, was a stream that we regularly drank from, when we were out walking or exploring. It was normal for everyone to drink from the streams when we were out. I remember once with this particular stream, I had a drink from it, and remarked it was especially good tasting. So everyone with me tried it, and we all agreed how good it tasted. We walked on past the septic tanks, and came across a dead sheep that was rotting in the stream. We all decided that was what probably made it taste so good!

College Farm had about a six foot high stone wall around the farmyard, with a five bar gate to get inside it. It was about a 100 yards from the gate to another small gate, with a small Ha-Ha about 30 feet from the house. (A Ha Ha is a ditch in the land, usually with a wall that comes to the level of the land that the building is on, protecting it from the animals that are in the adjoining field. As it is not visible from the house it is not unsightly).

In this field they kept some cows, but mostly they kept a gaggle of geese. I never stopped to count how many, just let me say there were too many! My mother used to send me there after the war, to get eggs from Mrs. Oakey, the farmer's wife. Before I entered the yard, I would look to see where the geese were - hoping they were at the far end of the field. I would open the gate very quietly, and close it the same way. Then I would take off running as if my life depended on it, which it did! The geese would come running straight for me, with their necks outstretched, making an awful hissing racket. This was another good practice for my 100-yard dash! I would crash through the small gate, slamming it behind me, and crash into the door, banging on it as hard as I could, to get Mrs. Oakey's attention.

She always helped me back, or let me go through the house to the other yard, so I could avoid the geese. One time I didn't get the small gate closed when I went through it, and the geese followed me in. They had me pinned against the door, stretching their necks towards my face. I just covered my face with my hands, and screamed bloody murder, until Mrs. Oakey came and saved me. I have never had a great love of geese!

Opposite College Farm, down the Station Road in Friar's Well, there was a sweet chestnut tree, that bore enough nuts for the whole village to use. Also there were plenty of horse chestnut trees for our conker games. Friar's Well always had plenty of edible mushrooms, just not as good as the ones Gramp gathered. It was also renowned for large clumps of stinging nettles, waiting for us kids to fall into.

A cure taught me by Gran for nettles stings, was to gather some dock leaves, rub the upper parts together to release the juices, spit on it, rub it together again and apply it to the sting. This will relieve the burning sensation, and it really does work. She said that is why the dock plants always grow plentifully around stinging nettles. It does seem to work out that way.

At the bottom of Friar's Well, against the wall, my uncle Alf had his pigsties. There were several, because that was how he made his living during the war. He was my grandparents' eldest son. His wife's name was Ada, but she was always called Pat. She came from London, and they never had any children. I know he worked with his pigs all day every day. He used to stop by Gran and Gramp's, on his way home for his dinner at noontime. He would come in and sit on the *chaise longe*, wearing his working Wellington boots that stank of pigs. We would say to him: "Alf your boots stink". He would always respond, "Ha! That's a bit of good stuff. It'll clear y'a 'ead out". He would never leave his boots outside, and Gran would say it is a waste of time complaining.

In that same area where Alf had his pigs, some years before, my grandfather used to keep chickens for market, selling eggs, and chickens for food. This was when my mother was a child. The story goes, according to Mum; Gramp decided it was time for her to learn how to kill chickens. Gramp showed her how to do it, by holding their bodies under her arm then holding the head, stretching it and twisting it at the same time. Apparently Mum did this to about half a dozen chickens, laid them down, and went to help Gramp gather the eggs. About half way through this job they heard this awful noise, and looked over to where it was coming from. There were these six chickens Mum had 'killed', running around with there heads dangling and flopping all over the place. Mum says she was so upset; she wouldn't ever go back down there again. All Gramp said was: "Dumb chickens they don't know enough to lay down when they are dead."

The bottom edge of Friar's Well had a high stone wall around it, and on the other side was Miller's Lane. This led to a couple of cottages and, at the far end, a large farmhouse and farm. There was a right of way through the field, to the trout stream, millpond, and the Souldern Mill. Souldern was the next village. If one followed the Trout Stream down to the right, it would take you to the Viaducts, and a swampy area that had all kinds of different birds and plants growing. If one followed the stream to the left, it would take you into the wooded parklands. Before you got there, there was a large pond that was hidden from view, because it was down a steep bank. There was about a ten to fifteen foot high waterfall that ran into it.

After the war we were told there were some really nice trout in the stream, and Gramp said when he was young he used to catch them by tickling their bellies. He told us we weren't really supposed to fish for them, because they belonged to the Cartwright's, and if we were caught doing it we would be in trouble, because that was considered poaching. If you were caught, first they would take your fishing rod away from you, and then whatever you had caught.

Well we didn't have any luck tickling their bellies, so we decided to try fishing for them at the base of the waterfall, that was well hidden from passers by. We used a three-foot long ash twig for a pole, which is very strong and supple, attached some fishing line to it, and a small float and hook. So if anyone took it, they wouldn't be getting much. In any case we left the pole hidden in the bushes, so we wouldn't be seen with it. When we went fishing, we always made sure we had at least two tops on so we could hide the fish inside our tops and that way they wouldn't be seen. Plus, we didn't have the fish touching our skin. We never did get caught and it was true, those were the best tasting trout I have ever eaten. The flesh was a very pale pink and so tasty.

Tennis Courts at the Park House

The Park Grounds wrapped around the rest of the village, behind Park House, the church, and all the way to the Bicester Rd or Upper Aynhoe Grounds. Behind the church was the old icehouse, and the lawn tennis courts, where many village children, including me, first learned to play tennis. The rest was mainly a wooded area, with nice paths for walking. In the spring, the whole area is covered with a blanket of snowdrops. Half way to the Bicester Road, was the walled gardens for the Park House. There they grew vegetables and flowers for cutting. They also had extensive glass greenhouses, so that they could pro-

Aynhoe Park House 1920's

duce tropical fruits and flowers for the Park House, even in the winter.

Just beyond the walled gardens and the Bothy - the name of the house for the gardener - was a bridle path to Souldern - part of Portway. To enter this there was a stone stile to step over. The path was very narrow, only about four feet wide, with very high stone walls on either side. These were probably eight feet high, which made the area very dark, damp, and ominous. This was just right for feeding children's imaginations. The whole path probably went half to three-quarters of a mile, before you came out into the field below. There the view was incredible, and at the right time of the year, there were masses of wild snowdrops and violets everywhere, just waiting to be picked.

Before one got to the field, the path had to be walked through, and this was not pleasant. Half way down it, there was a bridge that went over the path. That allowed the Park House vehicles to cross over. This bridge was so low, that the tunnel it formed allowed only the very shortest of people to stand up straight inside. The roof had all kinds of nasty things growing in it, and it stank even worse than the path did. Of course we children made it worse for ourselves, by telling each other all that we imagined had, or could have happened in the area. Everything came to mind, from a headless horseman, down to Trolls that were just waiting for us to appear. We did a lot of running down the path, but could not run through the tunnel because of the low ceiling.

If we walked to the edge of the village by the Bicester Road, we could cross over the Croughton Road, and go up second crossing to the fields where we picked potatoes. At the far end of the road, to the right across the potato field and beyond the farmhouse, were the Pest Woods.

The road that the Second Cross-ing Road ran into, was the Brackley Road, which also led to the village of Charlton. If one crossed over went into the next field, and then to the field to the right, once you got to the back of it, you would come to the old Roman Camp. The tunnel, that is supposed to go from the camp to the village, exited inside the second house my grandparents lived in when they were married. Gran said it was blocked up because the air was bad in it, and was therefore not safe to go into. She said some of it has probably caved in, because it was almost two thousand years old. She told me it is easy to see, because it has 2 very distinct arches, and is very high to allow a tall man to walk through standing up. I always wanted to go in and see the arches when I was a child, but the Bourne sisters lived there, and they always seemed to be unapproachable by small children with curiosity. I have seen the arches in recent years, and they are just like Gran de-scribed them. The house was thatched then, but is not any more.

Moat around Roman Camp

As we are back in the village, I will tell you of other places that were of interest to kids through the generations. Not just those of us during the war time years, because some things never change. At the top of the Station Road, the green there was where the stand was situat-ed, that the farmers put their milk cans on. This was for the dairy wag-on to pick them up, to take to the dairies for processing, and delivering to the people who lived in the cities. When the milk cans were gone, it was a great place to play statues. We would all get on the stand except for one person who would be "it". They would grab your hand, and pull you off, and however you landed, you had to keep that pose without moving a muscle. After all were pulled down, then the one doing the pulling would go around trying to get one of us to move. That is, with-out touching us. Whoever moved first, was then "it".

In the same area the village stocks were located. They were protected behind an iron railing. I don't know when it was that they stopped using them, but at one time they were used as a form of punishment. The last person to be placed in the stocks was a Wrighton. People were locked in them, so others could ridicule them for whatever they had done wrong. Sometimes they were even taunted, by having rotten fruit and eggs thrown at them. This was long ago, even before my grandmother's time.

Bottom village green before the road had tarmac

At the green at the bottom

Hill Trees - much loved by all the village children for many generations

of the village, across from College Farm, there was a bank of mostly very old elm and oak trees, that were known as Hill Trees. The bank was very steep, and probably rose about forty feet, and was about two hundred feet long. The trees were so old, and the bank so steep, the roots grew in such a way as to look like caves, with openings under the roots that went way back into the bank. They were great places to hide, and to watch the goings on around the area without being seen. None of us were allowed to play there, because they were classified as being 'very dangerous' and, from what I understand, they were classified as being 'dangerous', even when my grandmother was a child. I wouldn't be surprised if it didn't go back a couple of generations before that. But none of the trees ever came down, and as far as I know they hurt no one.

There were many generations of children that defied their parents and played there, and there were probably as many children got "good hidings" for playing there too. I know I got my fair share of them. The hidings are the only hurt I know that those trees might have caused! It wasn't too long after the war that they cut them all down, but left the roots in. So there was still a good place for kids to play, and still earn their "good hidings", because the roots were said to be dangerous still.

Blacksmith Hill is where the Blacksmith's forge was, for shoeing horses. Teddy Mobbs was the blacksmith. He loved children and they loved him too. We village children enjoyed going to watch him work, especially in the winter when it was cold outside. It was always toasty warm inside. He always had time to explain to us what he was doing, how it worked, and that it did not hurt the horses. In fact he said they liked it.

There were some very large families in the village, that weren't related to us. They were the Ayres, Williams and Garrett families, and they each had eight or more children. With those families, it seemed as if there was always a new baby in tow. Of course this helped to keep the school full, and gave us all more children to play with. The people in the village that I found the most interesting, were the elderly ones. I loved to spend time talking to them, and to hear what it was like when they were young.

There was a house on the left inside Betsy Wattses, which was the name of an opening in the wall near the top of the lane. Through that same opening, led to what used to be the infant school when Gran was a child. The house back there seemed to be a fair size. I only ever went into the front room/come kitchen. My mother says the problem with it was, that you had to go through each room to get to the next.

I believe all that lived there were related to Anne Shergold. There was the mother, Mrs. Garrett, known to all as "Granny with the pinna on". She was very old, and still wore the long black dresses, with the high white ruffle around her neck. She always wore a beautifully starched white pinafore (pinna), that tied at her waist, and went to about eight inches above the bottom of her dress. The material was of the kind, that allowed one to see the colour of her dress behind it. It had a design all around the edges, but it wasn't quite embroidery. Her whole attire was completely immaculate. She was supposedly in her nineties, and still washed herself every morning with the cold rainwater from her water butt. She did this summer and winter alike. In the winter she would break the ice off the top to get to the water. We were told this was the reason her skin was still perfect, like it was on the day she was born.

She had two daughters, Gert and May Garrett, that took care of their mother, the house, and an extensive garden. They grew lovely flowers and lots of vegetables. The way they earned their money, was by doing the ironing for the Squire's family at the Park House, including Lady Cartwright, the Squire's mother, who lived at the Grammar House. They did the ironing in a large wooden building, that was elevated off the ground, requiring you to climb about six steps to go inside. It was a large room with lots of windows, and a wood stove in the middle that had to run summer and winter alike. The reason for this was, that they heated the irons on the top of the stove. They were not very large irons, but very heavy because they were made of cast iron. The whole iron used to become hot, so to protect their hands they had pads similar to oven gloves.

Most of the laundry they had to iron was white, and seemed to be mostly linens, though they did do shirts for the Squire. They would show us the correct ways to iron the different linens, especially the ones for the dining tables. The folds would be like the folding of a screen. This would be for the table cloth and the serviettes. If the linen was damask, it took even greater skills to keep it in line. All of the linens were starched, and these had to be sprinkled, or dampened down with water, then rolled up before ironing could even start. I believe this is how Granny with the pinna on, had such perfect pinafores.

Taylor's House Lt to Rt Joan Taylor, Norah Parrish, Mrs Taylor 1936

Just down from my grandparent's home, is where Mr. and Mrs. Taylor lived. They were Anne Shergold's grandparents, and he was the signalman at the station. The house was set back from the rest, and didn't have any houses attached to it, but apparently it was two houses at one time. They had a large front garden and an even larger back garden, which was quite steep. In the front garden, against the wall of the house, besides the usual apricot tree that everyone else had, they had a peach tree that often bore a lot of fruit. This of course was a real treat for all, and Mr. Taylor shared them quite readily. Mr. Taylor also had a way with roses, and he grew all kinds. Each year on 25th June, when it was my Grandmother's birthday, Gramp would go down to Mr. Taylor's and buy a bunch of roses from him for Gran. During this time it cost him 2/6 (12 1/2 p).

Up from my grandparent's house was Miss Watt and Miss Dolby's house, right on Wembley Corner. This corner was very danger-ous traffic wise, with plenty of car accidents over the years. Their house was set back from the road. Their entire garden was in the front, and there was a wall half way down the garden, that was high enough to afford them some privacy.

What was interesting about them was, that they kept several beehives, and they would both willingly, and patiently, explain to us about bee keeping, and gathering the honey. During the war, to get to taste something sweet was a real treat for us children. Their garden was all flowers, probably for the bees.

At the northern end of the village square, lived John and Alice Howe. They were brother and sister. Their house and garden is very large and is unique. Though being in the centre of the village, it still has storage buildings and a garage. The house had the large ovens, which were available years ago, for the entire village to use for baking and roasting. It was known as the Bake House.

Up until shortly before the Second World War, it was strongly understood by all, that the entire village population was expected to at-tend church on Sunday mornings. Each family had their own pew, so any missing members were easily spotted. That is probably why the few times Gran took me to church, we always sat in the same pew even though there were many to choose from.

The one excuse that a family may have had for not going to church, was the need to cook the traditional Sunday dinner. This was almost always roast beef with all the trimmings. The roast was cooked in a slow oven for a long period of time. To make it possible for the entire family to attend church, all the families took their roasts in their own pans, marked accordingly for identification, to the Howe's to be cooked in their large ovens. After church, a family member would pick it up, while the rest of the family went home to start cooking the previously prepared vegetables.

Denis:
The roast dropper

The story told in my family went like this: it was Denis', their youngest sons turn to pick up the roast. He was in a hurry, because he had plans to play with his friends. He was running back with the roast, when it rolled off the pan, and landed on top of the drain in front of the village shop. He made sure no-one saw what had happened, so he quickly picked it up, brushed it off, put it back in the pan and took it home, not saying a word to any-one. Even as a child Denis was always very partic-ular about cleanliness. When it came time for dinner, he decided he wasn't that hungry and really only wanted a few vegetables, which was fine with the rest of the hungry family. It wasn't until Denis was an adult, that he felt it was safe to confess what he had done, and he finally told Gran and Gramp.

Back to John Howe and his sister Alice. She was another one that used to wear the long black dresses. She also piled her hair up high on the top of her head. I thought it made it look like a witch's hat! This would be another house I used to go to for eggs. I always hoped John would come to the door, not Alice, because she was very scary the way she stood so erect, and looked down at you over her nose. She probably had to do it that way because of her hair. Gran said; there was no rea-son for her to dress that way, as she was younger than her. Gran thought she was strange!

This is a story told to me by my mother. It happened when she was a child. Two Aynhoe men, Sam Judd and Rich Savings had been in Adderbury for the evening. They had spent most of the time at the local pub, and were quite drunk when they started for home. No one knew what got into these 'ol' boys' minds, but along the 3 mile walk back to Aynhoe, they took every gate along they way off its hinges, and laid them neatly in the middle of the road. In those days there was little to no traffic, so that wasn't the problem. The problem was, that almost all of the fields had animals in them. By the time they were discovered, there were animals everywhere except in the fields!

What they had done was the talk of the village. When Richard Cartwright heard what had happened, he saw the funny side of it all. Later, Richard told his Aunt, Beatrice Cartwright, the magistrate over in Brackley about it. She said the men really needed to be taught a lesson they wouldn't forget. She would have liked to open up the court to give them a real scare, but she and Richard worked out what he could do. Richard, and his former tutor, Bill Wightman, were to bring Rich Savings and Sam Judd to Brackley, with the men thinking they were going to prison for what they had done. The whole village added to it, by telling Rich and Sam that they'd probably be in prison for about 6 years. Some even said it could be as long as 10 years. Richard had a large car, and late one afternoon the two men were picked up, by him and Bill Wightman. They put them into the back of the car, and they drove them the long way round to Brackley. Neither of the men had probably ever been there before. By the time they got there it was dark, and by now the men were scared stiff as to what might happen. Richard and Bill made a big issue about getting them out of the car, and working out where to take them. Then, Bill turned to them and said, with as stern a voice as he could muster, "Now let this be a lesson to you two, next time you do something like that, you will go to prison. Now go home." They wanted to know how they were going to get home. They were told to figure it out for themselves, and walk! They were the laughing stock of the village for a long time. It took even longer before they were able to live it down.

Richard Cartwright used to like to have all the latest and best things for the village, along with, when possible, for himself to be the Captain of whatever he had purchased. One of his big projects was, the fire equipment and full uniforms for all the Firemen, including brass helmets with fancy topknots. Richard was the Captain, and they were all always hoping for a big fire,. They were usually disappointed, with most of the fires being just chimney fires and haystacks. The fire equipment was kept across the road from the Grammar House, in a building appropriately called the Fire Station. On one of the more memorable occasions, an alarm had gone off for a fire. Most of the men were in the pub, and were already almost three sheets to the wind. They loaded into the lorry, with most of them in the back. When they turned the corner, as they came out of the fire station, Tommy Humphris, who was already well up in years, and being in the very back of the lorry, fell out. He was too drunk to realise what had happened. When the rest of them got close to where the fire was, one of them said "Shame Tommy fell off, he had the lantern to show them where the fire was." They were all disappointed it was just another chimney fire. Richard said, "Pity the thatch didn't catch, and we'd have had a good one then."

Close to the Fire Station, Richard had a very large productive timber yard. This happened several years after the previous incident. Richard was in the Grammar House talking to Bill Wightman, when he looked out across at his timber yard and saw flames going up. He said "Bill, now we have a good one." It needed help from all the local area Fire Stations that included at least Deddington, King Sutton and Brackley. They all enjoyed it and the excitement. They considered it a first class fire, especially since it lasted, with the smoldering, for several days.

Aynhoe Fire Brigade in full uniform

During the war years fuel was rationed. Our only fuel was soft coal, and each household only received one hundredweight a week, which is not enough to heat and cook with. This was supplemented with wood. To do this we had to go "wooding". This would take you many miles from home. With our village being on the top of a hill, to get anywhere one goes downhill. Consequently we went down with empty arms, and came back up fully loaded. Usually when we went, which was a weekly chore, we went in group. Several women and their pre-school aged children. To make it as easy as possible, every imaginable thing we had, that could hold wood and had wheels, was used. Normally that would be a pram.

We would look for wood in hedgerows, especially if there were trees in them, in spinneys, or down in the Park Lands and any other wooded areas. We would only take fallen wood, because no one would want to damage the trees. If the word were out that a tree was being cut down, we would all go to the site. Though we wouldn't get the main part of the wood, there were always the large chips from the woodcutter's axe, and all the branches and twigs that came off when the tree fell.

I always thought it was a sad time when a tree was cut down; it looked so grand standing there so high. The women standing around watching, would comment on how old the tree must be, and how incredible for it to live so long. But it didn't stop the scurry for the wood when it was down. Each person would admire the next person's size of wood, or large chunks they were able to get. There would be

Brackley Road now Charlton Road 1936

comments like; this piece will take a good hour to burn, and; if I bank it up with coal and coal dust it will last even longer.

The Corner 1920-30

When my mother was a child, the women of the village needed to do the wooding, to help with the home heating and cooking. But none quite like a certain group of the village women. They were the women that lived up the Brackley Road and on the Corner; the Corner being the houses to the right of the Brackley Road, up to the bottom of Blacksmith Hill. The families that lived in that area, were the poorest, and usually had the largest number of children. The women were strong and course, but they worked hard to keep their families together, and to put food on the table. Their wooding skills put others to shame. They would travel further than most to find the largest pieces. They would load their arms with huge loads, and carry a large log on each of their heads. Mum said she never saw any of them drop them. One old fellow in the village saw them drop everything they had though. The way he told the story, to any villager interested in listening, and apparently the story got better

71

with each telling! He said he had stopped work to eat his lunch, when he spotted these women loading themselves up in the Park woods. What they hadn't noticed though, was that they were between the rutting herd of buck deer, and a herd of does. The bucks charged the women. The wood and logs went flying everywhere as they scrambled to get out of the way, through a wire fence that would not stay wide enough for them to get through, without showing all their unmentionables!

Set routines were practiced by most villagers, not just my grandparents. It was how they were taught from a child, and it showed a mark of accepting responsibility. One fellows routine was so exact, you could set a clock by what he was doing. He was known as Pudgy, but his real name was George Williams. Like many in the village he was of small stature, but he had one severe handicap - he had been deaf most of his life. He worked for Graham-Whites across from 20 Aynhoe, so Gran and Gramp saw his comings and goings daily. He worked from 7 am in the morning until 5 pm. Graham-Whites fed him his dinner each day. At 5pm he went home, had his tea, washed up and changed clothes, so that he was walking past the stocks, at exactly 6 pm each night, on his way to the Great Western Arms at the station. When he arrived there, his chair was beside the fireplace, with his freshly drawn beer waiting for him on the table beside his chair. No one was allowed to sit in his chair during his regular hours. The fire was always lit for him, winter and summer alike.

Hill cottages: The house and the hedge on the right is the one in the story in 1891

The next two stories took place in the 1890's. July 24th 1891 was a hot day, and two nine year old cousins, Ada and Mabel Wrighton, were hungry for fruit to eat. They both knew where the best supply could be had, because their grandfather David Wrighton was renowned for his fruit growing of all varieties, according to what was in season. He grew strawberries, raspberries, gooseberries, redcurrants and blackcurrants.

Ada lived in the last house on the left, at the top of Blacksmith Hill, on the edge of the village. She was the fourth, of six children, and the eldest daughter of Edwin and Eliza (Robbins) Wrighton. Edwin was a Master hedger and a water diviner; he could also read and write, which was unusual for men of his age in the village. He frequently scribed letters, or read correspondence for the villagers that didn't have those skills.

Mabel was the twelfth of fifteen children, of Edwin's older brother Henry and Julia (Borton) Wrighton. They lived at the station, and Henry made bricks and operated the brick yard located there.

Ada and Mabel together, used to clean house for their grandfather and his daughter Sarah, each week. Sarah was born with a deformity of her arms, making it impossible for her to do more than just care for her own personal needs. Sarah was known to be very dogmatic, and very much a no nonsense person, most children and many adults, were scared of her.

Ada thought that if they could get past Aunt Sarah, they could fill their pockets with a bumper crop of fruit, that was just right for picking. The house was the first house on the right, of the cottages known as Hill Cottages. There was a hedge that bordered the garden, and the path led to all the other cottages on the hill. Ada thought; if they could get to the hedge without being seen, they could crawl along low down beneath the window of the house that faced the garden, and make it to the fruit supply. All went well. They filled their pockets to overflow, and were about to go back the same way, when Aunt Sarah's thunderous voice boomed over their heads. "You girls thought I couldn't see you, well I have been watching you the whole time from the window. Now you get right into the house and empty your pockets onto the table; then skidaddle." The girls went right into the house, knowing it was a waste of time to resist her. They emptied their pockets of all the fruit, and was about to leave; when they noticed a curtain across the room that hadn't been there before. Typically, curiosity got the better of them, and they went to look behind it. To be stopped in their tracks, when Aunt Sarah curtly told them, "You girls stay out of there; my Pa is lying back there dead, waiting to be buried." They just looked at each other, and ran as if their lives depended on it

Because of her deformities, after her father died, Aunt Sarah was pretty much helpless. Normally, under these circumstances, she would have ended up in a workhouse, if no other family member could take her in. Instead the Cartwright's, being as they were, and always caring for the villagers, let her live in the house rent free. She interpreted this as giving her ownership of the house! With this elevated stature that she perceived; her behaviour was that of a person who ruled the village. When Sarah wanted anything, the villagers all jumped to her commands, and she commanded a lot! Digby Cartwright was the Rector of Aynhoe for many years. He was very considerate of all the parishioners – he was much loved and respected. After David Wrighton died, the Rector sent Sarah, from his own Sunday dinner table, a complete plate of whatever his family was eating, and usually enough for more than one meal. This was rushed to her by one of his servants, so that it was piping hot when it reached her table. She always inspected it before she let the servant leave. This particular Sunday, the meat was not to her liking. She told the servant, to tell the Rector that; in future she wanted her meat cut from the prime part of the roast, not from the scrub end like she had received that day. The servant knew he had to give the message to the Rector. Each following Sunday from that time on, when the Rector was preparing to cut the roast and serve his family he said, "First I have to cut the prime slices for Sarah, so it will meet with her approval." This continued until she died.

Jackdaws are birds very similar to crows but smaller. They make good pets and can be taught to talk. We always had plenty around Aynhoe. The best time to make pets of them, is just before they fly the nest. The only problem with that is, their nests are usually in the very tops of the trees. They used to nest in the tops of the elm trees, that went around the Big Butts. In the late twenties or early thirties, a bunch of Aynhoe boys decided they wanted some as pets. It was Arthur Butler, Arthur Page, Les Secult and Denis Parrish - my uncle. They climbed to the tops of the elm trees in the Butts, and got 5 baby Jackdaws. I don't know who ended up with 2 of them, but Denis only had one. The bird trained easily, and did learn a few words; he took a real liking to Gran. She would let him out of his cage each morning; he would fly through the house, as if to check everything out, then land on her shoulder. He would spend the bulk of the day perched there, chatting away.

When Gramps runner beans came into bloom, the bird would take breaks into the garden and eat all the red blooms. This did not please Gramp at all; being able to grow food was an important part of feeding large families. One morning the fishmonger, Sid Drinkwater from Clifton, came round. He told Gramp he was looking for a Jackdaw for a pet. If he heard of one he'd like to know about it. Gramp told him he just happened to have one, and he'd be glad to sell it him for 1/-. Mr. Drinkwater went off with the bird as pleased as punch, Gramp felt much the same way. It was only Gran that missed the bird. A couple of months later, Mr. Drinkwater offered to sell the bird back to Gramp for no more than he had paid for it. Gramp told him he wasn't interested. He then said: "George, did you know he has a liking for the runner bean flowers?" Gramp responded "Yes." Sid Drinkwater then called Gramp "A rotten bugger!"

Not too long after this incident, Sid Drinkwater could have got even with Gramp for what he did to him; but he didn't. Gramp, on a yearly basis, was hired by the Parish Council to count the traffic at Nell Bridge for 24 hours. During most of the nighttime hours, there was no traffic, and he didn't like to waste time; so he would fish out of the cut. At that time of the day, or night more specifically, it was classified as poaching. This one particular time he got an especially good catch of several trout. The next day Mr. Drinkwater stopped by the house, to see if Gran wanted to buy any fish. Denis spoke right up as children tend to do, when you least want them to. He told Mr. Drinkwater, "No, they didn't need any fish, because his Dad caught a whole bunch of bloaters in the cut the night before!"

Chapter 6
Life in War Time

Village life has always involved a lot of work, for all that live there. Lives revolved around work, whereas entertainment was generally whatever one could create. Mostly it took imagination, mixed with a little devilment. Sayings were a part of life, and there was a saying for just about every situation. There was also a large dose of superstitions and scare tactics, used to keep children from getting too venturesome. Added to this was a taste of guilt to make them tow the line.

The early 1940's and wartime in the villages, was different from living in the towns and cities. We did not have the real threat of bombing runs every night, and the consequent hours spent down in the shelter for safety. We were only exposed to that if we were making trips to the towns, especially if an overnight stay was planned. Just about all the rest of the hardships of war were present. And, of course, we knew what was happening in the towns, some of which could be observed from our village, as was the case during the blitz of Coventry. That bombing is my earliest memory. Though, because of being so young, and not knowing what it was, there was no fear attached to it, and was therefore seen from an entirely different perspective.

How I remember it; it was almost dark, but it was possible to be aware of other people around me. I seemed to be up high, and everyone there seemed to be very upset. However all I could see, besides shadows of the people, were all the pretty lights in the sky. There were blues, pinks, and yellows forming big coloured puffs. It was a long way off: all the way across the valley. I had the feeling that I was the only one liking it. One person there seemed to be doing something with her hands, and kept moving a ball around that she kept putting back under her arm.

Knowing what I know now, and from conversations with my mother, what was happening was the blitz of Coventry, on the night of November 14th 1940. Coventry is about 12 miles as the crow flies from our village. The reason I felt I was high up, was that I was in my mother's arms, and the people around us were other women, neighbours from our village. Considering what it was they were watching, it is understandable that they were upset. The lady who was doing something with her hands, was Gert Garrett. She was knitting, and the ball was the ball of wool that she kept on unwinding. She carried the ball around under her armpit. This was something I was to see her do for many years. Wherever she went, she was knitting, she would do it walking along and she never needed to look at it as she walked. This was a fairly common practice of all the women, especially in the 40's and 50s.

The rest of my memories of village life, during these early years, were more of awareness, and not in any special order. I was born in the Barrett Nursing Home in Northampton on 13th February 1940. I wasn't born at home, because my mother had Rheumatic Fever at the time. I was three weeks late and a breech. Eventually we did return to my grandparents' home, 20 Station Road Aynhoe, so they could continue to care for us.

During the war years, our village had an Army Regiment for the men and women. The women's was the ATS (Auxiliary Territorial Service Corps). We were used to seeing soldiers, both men and women in uniform. They would pass my sister and I playing in front of the house, stroke our hair and call June "curly", because of her curls, and me "Blondie". My mother did women's hairdressing and cut men's hair, so we were used to seeing the military people all the time.

One day a man came into our home, and put his gun in the corner by the cupboard. I was told not to touch it. He had on a soldier's uniform. He was tall, and when he sat down and I stood behind him, I remember he had dark curly hair. I do not remember anything else about him. Gran told me years later, that the next day I went down home, and told them this man slept in Mum's bed. They explained to me that it was all right, because he was my Daddy. This was the first time we had seen each other that I could remember.

During this time that he was home, I was about 2 years old and we went to Folkestone, for my sister's christening. Dad's family were all Navy people and originally from Hampshire, but had retired to Folkestone. Most of his brothers and sisters had moved there too. We got to meet some cousins,

Lt to Rt June, Norah, Syd, & Dawn Alsford Folkestone 1942

77

most were children, but one was older, his name was Neville Vaughan. He seemed to be very grown up to me.

He took me on my own to Dover, to see the sea. The beach was all pebbles. He pointed out the White Cliffs, and there seemed to be caves or openings at the base of them. Then he took me to the water's edge so I could paddle, and a wave came up and knocked me down. I was completely soaked. He said I couldn't go back on the bus all wet, so I took my dress off, and he put his jacket on me - it went down to my ankles. On the way back, people kept asking what had happened. He said I had made a big hole in the beach, and it would probably be there forever. It made me feel very proud of what I had done.

During this trip, I remember Grandpa taking me to get ice cream. It was the first time I had an ice cream cone, and I was told I

Agnes and Samuel Alsford 1942

had to eat it fast before it melted. These were the good memories of the trip, but there were some bad memories as well. The day we arrived, Grandma told me to go into the kitchen and see what was on top of the cupboard, which we were going to have it for dessert. I am sure looking back on it, she was probably very proud of being able to get such a treat for us. What she didn't count on was what I thought it was. I took one look into this large glass bowl, and thought I'm not eating those orange slimy slugs, and no body is going to make me, and I told her so. She got so mad at me, told me I was a naughty little girl, and if I didn't eat them, she would lock me in that dark garage, and the bombs would come down and kill me. I knew what that meant, and from what I remember I went berserk. I ended up in the living room on Grandpa's knee with him telling me stories. I don't remember having to eat the slugs, I don't think I did, (they were really sliced peaches in syrup). I never trusted or liked Grandma after that.

The next time I remember seeing my father, we had to go to Liverpool to see him in the hospital, because he had been injured in the war. My sister June was a toddler by this time. We were going to go by train to Liverpool, and were to stay with a family while we were there.

The only thing I remember about the trip, was waiting on the train station. It was very dark, and no lights were on because of the need for the blackout. Lights can be seen way up in the sky, which would tell the "Gerries", where to bomb us. All of a sudden there was a light across the railway tracks. A blackout blind had gone up which exposed this square window, with a lamp on the table in a dining car. I remember feeling the panic, as did everyone else around us. People kept shouting to get rid of the light.

Before it got dark at the station, I had noticed these metal things that had writing on them, and glass fronts, but they were empty. I asked Mum what they were. She said that before the war, sweets were put in them, and to get them out you had to put money in and turn the handle. I reasoned this must have been old fashioned, and in olden times, it wasn't that way anymore, because it was more modern now.

We went to see Dad in the hospital. He was in a big ward with other men that had been injured. June required some entertaining, so Dad said she could stand up behind him and gently brush his hair. She must be gentle because his head had been injured. June was doing fine, until she got bored, and had enough. She turned the brush around, and with the solid back of it, whacked Dad a good one on top of the head. After that, one of the other men took her off in his wheelchair, with her sitting on his lap. I guess Dad got over his injures because, if I remember correctly, he went back to the front.

I have one other memory of that trip. The people we were staying with had two boys, and they were reading a book with me. There was a picture of some flowers; they told me they were called Forget Me Nots. They said if I remembered them, and whenever I saw Forget Me Nots again then I would remember the two of them. I still do remember them, but I don't remember their names. I wish I did. My mother thinks their surname was Rivers. Apparently, when Dad was injured for the last time, he was half way up Italy after an earlier landing in Sicily. This was after he had left North Africa for the European invasion. He was sent home, and by the time he recovered from that injury the war was over. Many years later, he would still have blackouts, for no apparent reason, and go down like a board to the ground. Sometimes he would grab your hand before he fell.

Aynhoe was on the main London to Birmingham road, so a lot of the war equipment and supplies came through our village. There was a constant stream of Army trucks, and tanks travelling the road through the village. They made a lot of noise on the tarmac. There were several military stations all around us, and a lot of military people, besides the Regiment billeted in Aynhoe. When the Americans finally came into the war, a lot of American bases were added. We were told Americans called each other "Chum", and if we stood at the side of the road, and called out "Got any gum, Chum", they might throw sweets to us, if they didn't have gum. We really didn't want the gum; we wanted the sweets, because there was very little of them around. The American soldier's sweets weren't rationed. Each night my mother would have us stand in front of her, and she would give us each a teaspoonful of condensed milk. That was our sweet for the day. I still like a spoonful every now and again.

If the fruit couldn't be grown locally, we didn't have any. We had apples, plums, damsons, pears, strawberries, blackberries, gooseberries and apricots. Our village soil has a lot of lime in it, which apparently apricots like, so they grew prolifically.

Many years ago the squire had an apricot tree planted at each house. There is a sometimes disputed story, which is; that the reason for the trees was, so that each tenant could give part of their crop to the Park House, for the squire's family to use. This was supposedly to pay for part of the tenant's rent; the rest was for the families to eat. The squire had 27 of his own apricot trees so it probably isn't true. The Cartwright's were always generous to their tenants. It would not be like them to give in such a way. When the first apricot of the season arrived, my mother would pick it, split it in half, and give half to my sister and the other half to me. They were very large, about the size of a large orange, and very juicy. After we left the village and I saw other apricots so little and so hard, I thought there was something wrong with them.

The first time I ever saw a banana, was towards the end of the war. Mum sat me on her lap, and said she had something special for me, that it came from a long way away and was called a banana. She showed it to me, and then started to peel it. Bananas have a unique and distinct smell, and I wasn't about to have any part of it. Mum tried to persuade me to try it, but my stubbornness held true to form. It was years before I would eat them.

The rationing in Britain was very severe, as it was in all of Europe. There was very little, if anything, that had to be bought, that wasn't rationed. Mum would do peoples hair just for rationing coupons, so she would have extra coupons to get stuff for us children. Some of the items people just didn't buy; Mum would get those, and then swap them for another coupon that she could use.

Sometimes a farmer's wife would have their hair done, and they would bring some food from the farm for payment. I remember one incident vividly. The only eggs we could get from the store, were ones with a stamp on the side. Sometimes they were OK, but other times they were bad. Mum used to say they didn't taste like real eggs. This particular day, Mrs. Oakey came to have her hair done, and she brought three fresh eggs for us. Mum told me to be very careful, and to take them downstairs one at a time, put them in a separate bowl from the other eggs, and we would have them for our tea.

Well of course I thought I could carry them all down at once. I put my thumb through one of them. I was so scared, I thought Mum would surely kill me if she found out, or at the very least give me a good hiding. So I took the egg outside to the dustbin that had the ashes from the fire in it and buried the offending egg. I went in and put the other eggs in a bowl. I searched through the shop eggs to see if I could find one, that had a stamp that was not complete and faded. When I found one that suited, I gently rubbed it with carbolic soap, (the only kind we had during the war), until the mark could be barely seen. I put it in the bottom of the bowl with the others, and hoped Mum wouldn't notice. I had a rough time for a few days but she never knew.

While Mum did her hairdressing, Gran took care of us. In the early years I remember very little about it, except that if Gran called us to come into the house for any reason, we had better come on the first call. If we didn't she wouldn't say anything, she'd just stand at the door with an ash twig in her hand - well we knew we were going to get it across the legs, as we passed her going through the door. She would only swish it once, but her aim was dead on. We would stand back from her as far as we could, to get a running start, all the time trying to persuade her to give us another chance. She would say; you know I only call you once. We would start with the "But Granny", in the meantime, trying to work out a strategy to avoid the swish. Nothing ever worked. What we tried most often was the high stepping method. Even with that she would only catch us the once she intended. Well, did it sting! It usually worked for a considerable length of time, and until we got to playing with something we just couldn't leave right away.

One survival chore involved the blackout curtains, that were carefully sealed around the windows each night. My responsibility was to close them, then go outside to make sure that not even a crack of light showed through. If a light showed through the window, it could be spotted by a 'Gerry' flying over, making it easy for him to drop a bomb on us. Another chore was the water to be used in the home. The water used for cooking, washing, and cleaning came from the pump, and this was carried each morning and afternoon by the bucketful, usually two buckets at a time.

Denis carrying water 1950's

Norah at the pump 1938

The drinking water had to come from the spring in Oakey's farmyard, located next to their big manure heap. Gramp said it was all right; that there was no way the manure could get into the water, because the spring was three to four feet up. Anyway village people had been drinking it for hundreds of years, and people in our village live to great years, so there can't be much wrong with it. Our house was about a quarter of a mile from the spring; Gran's a little less. But some poor people lived much further, because the spring was at the farthest point north in the village.

We used to be able to tell who had recently gone for water, by the pattern of the water splashes on the ground. One in particular, who spilled a lot, always left a large splash in front of Molly Berry's house.

That was Mr. Jeacock, Lady Cartwright's chauffeur. He always walked along with a violet ,or a piece of grass gripped between his teeth. Gramp used say "I'd be surprised if he gets back home with much left in his bucket". Gran would say "It's a waste of time him going for it".

Another chore that I hated was to go 'rabbiting'. When it was harvest time, we had to go down to the fields to catch the rabbits. Villagers, mostly children, would form a half circle around the combine harvester, each holding a big stick. We would wait for the rabbits to come running out, and whoever was closest would run after it, and try to hit it on the head to kill it. This was to supplement our limited meat rations. I hated to do it. Firstly I hated the taste of rabbit, and secondly I thought the rabbits were cute, and when they were skinned they looked like a naked baby to me. But, most importantly, I wasn't strong enough to kill them with the first blow - it took considerably more. Most especially I did not like the sensation of the shudder that went through my arm, when the stick connected with the head of the rabbit. So I used to miss it on purpose, or not run fast enough to catch it.

Years later, when all the rabbits had been purposely infected with myxamatosis to reduce their huge numbers, I did go into the fields and hit them over the head - to put them out of their misery. I hated to see what was happening to them, but I was also glad that I would never have to eat them again.

The other foods we got out of the fields, were the blackberries in the hedgerows. We would take them home, and Gran would make the best blackberry jelly, and blackberry and apple pies. We would also go mushrooming. The fields around us always gave a bountiful crop. It was necessary to go first thing in the morning, while the dew was still out, to get the best tasting ones. They were all sizes, from the size of an old English penny, to the size of a dinner plate, which could barely fit in a frying pan to be cooked. Gramp had a special mushroom patch. He would go to it very early in the morning, after he had started the fire, but before it was time to get Gran up. When we came downstairs he would say; we could have a nice plate of mushrooms fried in butter for breakfast. Then he would carefully take them out of the bag, and place them gently on the table for us to admire. There would always be one especially large that would warrant special praise. Gran would say she didn't think she had a pan big enough to cook it in. These mushrooms if cooked in butter, then served with homemade bread, toasted in front of the hot coals of the fire, are something to die for. Gramp would never tell us where his mushroom patch was. I tried many times to walk his speed and to go distances, allow for picking time, and walk back in the time he took, still no luck. I used to ask him if he would tell me where it was before he died. He said he would. He didn't!

Most families, during this period and before, maintained a pig for their extra meat. Gramp had two pigs, in a pigsty, that he kept in the back corner of his allotment, located up Blacksmith Hill. He always called his pigs Sally and Sarah, and usually cried when they had to be slaughtered. The allotment belonged to the house Mum was living in; Gramp grew vegetables there as well. He used to go up daily, to feed the pigs with cooked pigswill, left over food, potato peelings, etc. I would sometimes go with him and he would show me how the pigs liked to have their backs scratched with a birch broom. Occasionally I would get to do it. When the pigs were fat enough, then Arthur Payne or John Howe would come and do the deed. I never saw Gramp's pigs killed, but I did help with the killing of Joe Watts' pigs. Probably because his daughter Janet was my friend. She had to help, so I helped her. We would also get the balloon afterwards. This is a bit gruesome in today's time, but this was the early 1940's, and survival was always paramount.

Joe Watts was skinny, tall and lanky. He had a strange sense of humour, especially where children were concerned, but we all liked him. His farm hand was Derb Ayers, also a very nice person. The killing time would start off, with Joe Watts going in the pigsty, to pick out the pig to be killed. He would tie a piece of rope around one of their back legs then he would let him out of the sty. The pig would take off screaming bloody murder, and Joe would go running after him, his legs and arms going everywhere, trying to hang on to the rope. He would be bent nearly in half. He would be yelling at Derb to do something, besides standing there laughing like a bloody fool!

Eventually the pig would slow down, and be worked over to the low bench where it was to be killed. On the other side of the bench was a pile of straw. Once the pig was on the bench, Janet and I had to hold on to its back legs tightly. Joe and Derb held onto the front legs - the pig was still screaming like crazy. Then Arthur Payne would stick the big knife in and cut its throat length wise. The pig would give out one last blood-curdling scream, then silence. I never looked at the top end, and always wished I could cover up my ears 'til it was over. Once that part was done, then we had to rock the pig back and forth to get all of the blood out. At this point someone would set fire to the pile of straw behind the bench, I don't remember if the pig was cut open at this point or not. I don't think it was. The pig was then tipped onto the straw, to burn all the hair off it. After the fire burned out, it was ready to dress it out. Mum says, when she was a little girl, she used to like to pull the pigs toenails out and eat the meat that was behind them. The fire had cooked them to a turn. I thought that sounded horrible.

Now came the part that Janet and I had been waiting for, they cut the pig fully open and took out our balloon. They emptied the liquid out of it and gave it to us. We promptly put it in our mouths and took turns blowing into it, until it was fully inflated, and then someone would tie a string around it to keep it up. These balloons would last us a good six months. The whole time we were working on this the men would be laughing, we thought it was because they were happy for us. Years later I knew why they were really laughing. It was because we were unknowingly blowing up the pig's bladder and what they had just emptied out was its urine.

Chapter 7
Working With Gran.

"Some people turn up their sleeves to work, and others turn up their noses." This was my favourite of all Gran's sayings, and she had many. This was also the one I heard the most. Gran used to say, "A girl wasn't worth her salt if she couldn't cook, sew, knit, and it was additionally nice if she could crochet as well." Gran was definitely not going to allow her eldest granddaughter not to be worth her salt. So my education began at a very young age, though it was always done in a most positive way with ongoing encouragement.

Each morning, the large white scrubbed table in the main room, was stripped of its tablecloths, and the surface was prepared for the day's work. If we were to clean brasses or silverware, then a newspaper was put on it to protect the wood. If it was the time for ironing, and this was always on Tuesdays, old blankets were folded to make a thick pad, followed by a couple of old sheets, folded on top to give a good ironing surface. This was done mainly to protect the table from being scorched by the hot iron. Other times Gran's sewing machine came out. It was a table model that had a handle on the right side, which was turned to make the machine sew. It was primarily black, with very decorative designs and lettering on it in red and gold. It was a brand called "Leo". Gran used to tell me how she made all my mothers dresses, plus all the clothes for her five sons along with Gramp's coats, jackets, trousers and shirts. Sometimes she would work so late at what she was making, that she would fall asleep at the machine and only wake up when the daylight came through the window. Gran was able to make any article of clothing she wanted, without having to use a pattern. Our eldest daughter Jane has been lucky enough to inherit that skill from her.

Gran taught me to sew on that old machine of hers, and I learned well enough to receive compliments on my sewing skills. Years later I bought myself an electric sewing machine, but it took me a long time to figure out what to do with my right hand, now that I didn't have to turn the wheel on the side. Gran also taught me how to do all of the hand stitching, running stitch, backstitch, French seams, facings and blind hemming stitch. When I was seven, I made a yellow gingham gored skirt, that had a square bib in the front with cross over straps into the back all, done in hand stitching. Later, I entered it in an adult hand sewing competition, at our village garden fete, and I won a second prize for it. The whole family was very proud of me.

The table was also used to prepare the meals. If it was the day to do the baking, then all the equipment that was going to be used was brought from the pantry and put on it, along with all of the ingredients. Gramp would get the fire going in the grate, so the oven would be at whatever temperature Gran needed, depending on what she was going to make. She had a very large square pastry board and rolling pin, that she used when making pies. Gran would get the mixture ready for the pie crusts, but before she added the water, she would show me how to work the flour and lard with my fingers, so it felt and looked like bread-crumbs. Only then was it considered ready for the water. It was impor-tant for the water to be very cold, and this was the only time you would stir anything with a knife. This was so one didn't stir all the air out that you had just put in during the time you were working it to be like bread-crumbs. "If you stir with a knife, you stir up strife" was another of Gran's sayings.

Then came the rolling out, and making the right size shapes, de-pending on what you were planning to make. I would turn up my sleeves as hard as I could for this part. But between my skinny arms, and clothes that were two sizes too big (to make them last), keeping the sleeves turned up rolling out pastry, was next to impossible. Of course, just as Gran would walk back into the room, my sleeves would be down by my wrist, and she would say; "Tut-tut Dawn, some people turn up their sleeves to work, and others turn up their noses." I'd say; "Gran, I really did turn them up." And she would always respond; "If you had done it right the first time, they'd still be up there now." That is why I knew that saying so well, because I never quite got it right.

What really impressed me about Gran's cooking skills, was that she could peel apples, for an apple pie, without the peel breaking. She told me I would be able to do it one day, when I had as much practice as she had. I was well into my adult years before I could do it consistent-ly. I am proud to say though, that by the time I was eight, I could cook just about anything I was asked to, including complete meals.

Because all the surface cooking was done over ~~the~~ open flames, the outsides of all the saucepans, frying pans, and kettles, were covered in thick soot. So one had to be careful never to touch your clothes, or the furniture, or put them down on the table. When you washed them, they had to be held out of the water, and the inside washed while being held over the pan. Gramp always took the pots and pans up to the washhouse to clean them. He was always the one to wash them.

When I was about four years old, I used to sit on a stool just in front of the arm of Gran's chair, as she taught me to knit. There she taught me the basics of knitting. She would do the "hard parts" first; so I could get used to the easier tasks. Then she would let me try the harder parts. Gran would cast on for me, and then do the first 4 rows to get me started, and I would do the plain or garter stitch. She would pick up the stitches I dropped, or eliminate the stitches I had inadvertently added. She advanced me on to stocking stitch, which meant doing the purl stitch. I had the hardest time with that one, so she would start and finish the row for me, and I would just do the middle.

While I was doing, or rather struggling with this, Gran would be knitting at the same time. During the time I was knitting my row, or part of a row Gran would knit two or three. Depending on what she was doing, she never, or rarely, looked at her work. I used to say; "I wish I could do it like you", and she would always respond; "You will one day, it just takes practice." I hoped that would be true but sometimes, when I was really struggling, I found it hard to believe. As time progressed, I was able to do all the stitches, and I had progressed to making sweaters for myself. Gran showed me how to hold the needles and yarn, so you don't have to take your fingers off them to wind the wool around. Once I learned that method, I really started to speed up, and now I can say she was right; I can knit as fast as she did, and I don't have to look at my work either. Now, with all those skills accomplished, Gran could rest easy, because I was worth my salt.

There were other things Gran taught me. Like what to do with the pig's meat after it had been killed. Not that I still remember how to do any of it. Most of the time, I would just watch her, and she would always explain what she was doing. She would say; the only part of a pig you can't eat, is its squeal, everything else is usable. She and Mum relished the trotters (feet); Gran would not share the Tom Hodge- that is the testicles - with anyone. She let me have some of the chitlins - I believe those are the intestines cooked down - and the crackling - the skin - to chew on after it roasted.

What I loved most was, after she had finished rendering it down, you got large bowls of pure white lard, as smooth as glass. When it was set, Gran would cut me a thick slice of home-made bread, spread it thickly with this fresh lard, and a little of the brown jelly from underneath. Then she would sprinkle a little salt on it and give it to me to eat. She would always say "That will warm you inside and out."

One day when I went 'down home', Gran said she was glad to see me, because she had a big job to do, and she didn't like to do it alone. I was just who she needed to help her. She said, "Your Mum used to help me with this when she was a little girl, and now you are just the perfect size to help." It could only be done on days that were perfectly still, with no chance of a breeze coming up. We had to first shut all of the windows in the house, and lock all the doors so no-one could come in, and Gramp knew better than to open anything up. In fact, he stood guard to see everything remained still!

This completed, we went upstairs to Gran and Gramp's bedroom. There, all the furniture was pushed back to the walls, and in the middle of the floor was their feather mattress. Beside it a brand new ticking, sewn and ready for the feathers. The plan was; to undo the end of the old mattress, and transfer all the feathers into the new one. This should be done without having the feathers blowing everywhere. This was a precision job, that was planned out with no sudden moves, and most especially no heavy breathing or sneezing! The job was completed without a hitch, but it did take the best part of a day. Getting the bulk of the feathers transferred was relatively easy. Just a matter of putting the new ticking over the end of the old ticking, and pushing the feathers through very gently. The part that was time consuming, was getting the large amount of stragglers to release from the old ticking, because of the static electricity, and getting them into the new one.

Another thing I was shown, was how to put eggs in isinglass, so we would have eggs to eat even when the hens stopped laying. Gran said it stopped them from going bad, but I don't know how it worked.

We, of course, had the marble slab instead of refrigerators for the perishables. In the summer, when it was hot, some things were put into a bucket of cold water; to give it added protection from the heat. Maintaining a home during these early years was hard physical work, and a full time job, with very few luxuries to enjoy.

Chapter 8:
Gran and her Stories.

Gran told stories all the time. It probably helped that I was forever asking questions, and always wanted to know more. I have an insatiable amount of curiosity, so between the two of us we were a perfect combination. These stories were told when we were working, going for walks, knitting, sitting by the fire or, the best of times, when I was laying in Gran's hole in the bed, while she was getting washed and dressed in the mornings. The stories were told to me randomly, so I am going to tell them in much the same way - as they come to my mind.

Gran said our family were Wrightons, and they had been in the village for over 300 hundred years. Gramp wasn't from Aynhoe. In our village the women tended to stay, and the men come in from other places. So there are many different last names, but we are mostly all related. This made it hard on strangers to the village, as they could talk about someone to another person, and be unaware they were talking to a relative. It was kind of fun for those of us that were from there.

Gran was born in Aynhoe, at the top of the Blacksmith Hill, which at that time was the easternmost edge of the village. She was given the name Ada Fanny Wrighton. When she was fully-grown, she was only four feet eleven inches tall, and wore size four shoes. She came from a long line of Wrightons to be born in the village, and because there was no birth control at that time, most had large families. Her father's name was William Edwin Wrighton - he was called Edwin. He was a master hedger and notable water diviner. Gran said he could find water when no-one else could, and was therefore in great demand. He also had an allotment in the field, across the top of the first crossing, at the edge of the village. He apparently spent some time as a member of the Parish Council. He was six feet tall and had a white 'mutton chop' type beard. Her mother, Eliza Robbins Wrighton, was born in the neighbouring village of Clifton, but most of her relatives lived in and around Northampton. She too was very tiny - less than five feet tall.

Gran used to say her parents so idealized each other, that they didn't need children to be happy. Indeed, they would have been perfectly happy without them. She said they were good loving parents, but they were totally wrapped up in each other. That was why when he died, and they were carrying his coffin downstairs, she flung herself on the coffin and said; she wasn't going to let them stick him in the dirt. She passed out, never regained consciousness again, died two weeks later, and was buried next to him in the churchyard.

This story is about Gran's mother, Eliza, who had an elderly Aunt - Mary Wellings, who lived at Far Cotton near Northampton, and owned a lot property there. Each week Eliza would walk to her Aunt's home, which was at least 30 miles away, to clean house and to bake enough food for her to last a week. Sometimes she was so tired, that on her way back; she would fall asleep under the hedgerows. This Aunt was quite well off, and she used to tell her that, when she died, she would be well taken care of. When she died she left my great grandmother two things, one of which I remember was a kettle! All her money, houses and other belongings went to an organisation for the protection of cats! Gran said her mother was just very hurt. She said she didn't do anything for the money. She would rather have had nothing than what she got. Gran being a little feistier thought it was an insult!

When Gran was two years old, she said she pestered her father to let her go to school. At that time they didn't start until they were three. He talked to the teacher, and they agreed she could go, if he would pay ha' penny a month for her to attend. He agreed. Gran said she was very lucky, because most families couldn't have afforded to do that.

The infant school, at that time, was at the top of The Lane on the right, and to get to it you had to go through the gap in the wall - 'Betsy Wattses'. She said that, the places where they sat were like steps going up against the long wall in the room, and they held their slates on their knees to write the lessons. The teacher's desk was in front of the seats; this way the whole class could be seen at a glance. In infant school they learned reading, writing, arithmetic and the scriptures. They didn't learn history, geography, and literature, until they were in the big one room schoolhouse. On Gran's 6th birthday, she was told by her teacher that she now belonged in the big school; she told the teacher she knew her way there. The teacher told her to knock on the door, and when the door was answered, to tell the person answering it who she was and how old she was. When she arrived at the school she did exactly as she was told. She said "I am Ada Fanny Wrighton and I am 6 years old to-day." The teacher told her, that she had better come in then, because that was where she belonged. John Howe, who was a little older than Gran, used to say how he remembered Gran doing that, and how tiny she looked, but also how proud she was. They went to school all year until they were eleven years old. At that time the boys usually went to work in the fields, or learned a trade as an apprentice. The girls could also learn a trade like millinery, seamstressing or go into service, as a maid or as a cook.

Gran went into service with a family called Fortescue's, as an upstairs maid. He was a lawyer in Banbury, some six miles away. Gran had one half day off a week, and that never changed the whole time she was there, which was about eleven years. She did not leave until she married my grandfather. Gran said they were good to their staff, and always treated them very well. Their house is now the Whately Hall Hotel; it was very grand.

There are two stories she told me about her time there. Gran used to run the bath water for Mr. Fortescue. They had running water, and there was a wooden box around the tub. This box was about three inches higher than the top of the tub, and the tub always took a long time to fill. This particular day Gran turned the water on, then went down to the kitchen to get something. While she was there, she stopped to talk to the cook, and then remembered the tub. She ran upstairs, and was relieved to find the water just to the top of the wooden rim; she let some of the water out, and then told Mr. Fortescue his bath was ready. She went down to the dining room, that was directly under the bath-room, to find about a foot of water in it. She was so scared of what was going to happen to her.

The carpet in the dining room, when it was taken out for its an-nual spring cleaning, took ten men to lift it. She said she just knew she was going to loose her job. The outcome was; it took over a week to get the carpet and room cleaned and dried out, and many more than ten men to do it. What happened to Gran? She was told she had received enough punishment, just the thought of what she had done, and the work she had to do to help in the cleaning. She didn't need anymore problems, but she was told not to talk to the cook in the future, until all her work was finished.

The other story from there, was when Gran mistakenly made a date with my Grandfather to meet him at one end of the street, and to meet someone else at the other end. The two men could each see each other from where they stood. Gran kept hoping that one of them would leave, so she could go out with whoever was left, because this was her only time off for the week. Neither of them left, so she never got to go out. She said she made sure she never did that again! I said; "Gran. Fancy you doing something like that!" I always had the notion that ladies in long dresses were always very proper; but this wasn't the case. Gran said, "Oh, I've had my day" - she never elaborated on that statement! Later I asked Gramp why he didn't leave. He said that he knew that the other fellow was waiting for Gran. He was not going to be the one to leave and leave the path clear for him. Wenching was a serious business!

When Gran left Fortescue's to get married, they gave her a complete set of bone china dishes. She said there were over 80 pieces in the set. I have the last remaining cup and saucer from it. It is white, with a delicate green pattern on it; the edge of the cup is scalloped.

When she was very young, she said the stagecoach came through Aynhoe once a week, on its way from London to Birmingham. All the children would run to the bottom of Hollows Road, now called Hollow Way, and sit on the large bottom step of the house close by, so they could watch it go past and wave at the driver. Hollow Way is much the same now as it was then - a

The women are standing on the large step Gran sat on to watch the stagecoach go by

single track road, except that it has tarmac instead of dirt. It was the shortest route through the village, past the Cartwright Arms, through the Square, and down Hollow Way to the Banbury Road. Years later, after the first man had walked on the moon, Gran said; "You know, that is something to think about. In my lifetime we have gone from one stagecoach a week, to a man walking on the moon." It is true. These were incredible changes to adjust to in one lifetime.

Gran told me about another activity, which attracted a lot of the children's attention when she was young. It was the time when the local butcher was slaughtering the animals. The butcher was another Oakey; she said he had lots of children, 11 each of boys and girls. The shop was attached to the front of his house, and surrounding that was the yard that he slaughtered the animals in. The wall surrounding it was low - about four feet high. This is where the children would sit to watch the slaughtering. There was a small building facing to the left of the house, where he would hang the meat to age, before being sold to the customers. What I couldn't understand, was the area allotted for the slaughtering was so small. I could not imagine being able to kill anything, of any size, in such a small space. Gran said they didn't have any problem, and that Mr. Oakey was a very skilled slaughterer and butcher.

Gran used to make a lot of home-made wine. She would make it in barrels, and when it had finished fermenting, carry it to the attic to age. This particular time, as the story goes, she had some elderberry wine fermenting. She thought it was close to being finished, so she kept listening at the opening in the top of the barrel throughout the day. Finally she heard no sounds in the barrel, so she corked it and looked for Gramp to help her carry it upstairs. He was nowhere to be found, so she got Mum to help her. Well she said, imagine her surprise when they went to lift it! She said she could have lifted it on her own. The barrel was completely empty. They went looking for Gramp, and found him up the garden path, out cold, sleeping off all that wine. She left him there, and said it was three days before he came to. Gran vowed never to make wine again, she kept that vow!

Another time, Gran sold fireworks to earn extra money. What she didn't sell, she would box up, and save for the next Guy Fawkes Day. She kept them in the attic. Gramp had gone up there one day, probably looking for wine. Some time later, there was all this commotion, with jumping jacks going off down the stairs; followed by the whizzing of Catherine wheels. Plus other banger type fireworks; all being sent on their way by a very intoxicated Gramp. Before I was born, as you can tell, Gramp had a real drinking problem; he used to say it was his Irish blood that made him do it. The story goes that after he saw his first grandchild, my cousin Tony, while others say it was his first granddaughter, me, he vowed never to drink again. Instead he was

95

going to eat Sharps Toffees, and that is why we would always get toffees to eat when we went down home. He kept his word for the rest of his life; except for an occasional glass of brandy, for medicinal purposes.

Gran's house was one of the few houses in the village, that had a telephone during the war. It was there because of the hairdressing business Mum operated in the small upstairs room. It was the kind that had a round base with a dial on it. then a long stem, similar to a candlestick, with a speaker you were to talk into. On the side hung a tube that you held to your ear. Gran would not touch it, much less use it, she said it was all "witchery". Years later, when I was leaving to go to the States, I asked Gran if she would talk to me on the phone if I called. She said; "As much as I love you Dawn, and you know how much I do, I cannot talk on one of those things, not even for you." She never did!

I always thought Gran was way ahead of her time in her ideas, especially considering she was born in 1882. One example of this was, a belief she had about who was superior - men or women. Forget equality - that wasn't even considered. She believed women were the superior of the two sexes, and she backed this up with this reasoning; bearing in mind she had little knowledge of hormones. In any case, she would have probably said that proves her point.

According to Gran, one just has to look at a man with their harder muscle structure, and all the hair they have on their bodies, to realize they are closer to the animal kingdom than women. Women are more refined. They have smoother bodies, less hair, therefore definitely at the highest point in the evolutionary scale. In addition, women were generally more intelligent than the men. Girls always do better in school than boys, especially in the earlier years. The reason it changes later on, is because girls realise it is important for boys to think they are better, so they let them go ahead. To a woman that isn't so important, because women know they are better, and letting the men think that they are better keeps them happy. The next reason is because women can withstand more pain and discomfort than men do; childbirth alone proves that, because even if men could physically have children, they would not be able to tolerate the pain. Her next reason was, women can stand isolation better than men; that is why there are more widows than widowers, because God knows men cannot deal with it, or function

96

alone, as well as a women can. She always added that is a known fact. (Later on when they started the space programs, she used to say; it's the women that should be doing it, not the men, because men can't stand that much isolation). The final reason was, that it is really the women, for the most part, that run the house, raise the children and make the home finance decisions. The women do it, but let the men think they are the ones in charge, again because of the men's egos. Women don't have to keep being patted on the back; they just know they are the best. She also said that most men couldn't see a job if it was to come up and bite them.

We would talk about the things I would like to be able to do that I couldn't. Once, I wished I could either sing in tune, or at least to be able to whistle. It was well known that I couldn't carry a tune in a brass bucket, and that has never improved. But, I thought that; if I could just whistle it would be something. Gran told me her father used to say; "A whistling girl and a crowing hen, was neither fit for God nor men." So I shouldn't worry about it. That information really didn't help though!

Chapter 9:
Gramp and His Stories.

Gramp was born in Poona, in the East Indies, on 7th September 1877, the 5th child of his family, who were all born in different parts of the East Indies. Three younger siblings were born in the Banbury area, after they returned. One sister subsequently died as a child. His father was stationed in the East Indies with the army. He had joined the Oxford Militia at sixteen, then in 1856, when he reached what was classified as the correct age, he was transferred to 49th Foot 1st Battalion Princess Charlotte of Wales. In January 1858 he transferred to 2nd Foot 1st Battalion Queen's Royal. His father's name was Alfred Parrish, who was born in Knight's House, between Croughton and Cottisford, just over a mile from Aynhoe. He was listed as being 5 ft 8 at time of his discharge from the army; his wife was reportedly very short.

After he retired from his military service, he took up market gardening in Grimsbury, close to Banbury. His wife was from Drissey, about five miles outside the Irish city of Cork. Her name was Mary O'Keeffe Parrish. She was an ardent Catholic, and apparently a tough task-master - about five feet tall. Gramp said there was very little kindness or warmth about her, and she was very domineering.

When Gramp married Gran, because Gran was not a Catholic, and they were married in Aynhoe Church, his mother had Gramp excommunicated from the church. I fixed that though before Gramp died. I got the priest to come up and reinstate him. Gramp's name was George Edward Parrish. When he was young he had fair hair, but it went white at a very young age.

Gramp was still a baby when he came to England. Even so, by the time he left, he said he was used to the Indian heat and strong sun. I think that was another one of his "stories". He never thought the sun was much good in England - rather fickle. So he called it "feebie", referring to it being feeble. The reason for this, he maintained, was if you called it the sun, it would know you were talking about it, and would hide behind the clouds. If you called it feebie, it didn't realise you were talking about it, and would stay out. He never seemed to be able to get enough of the sun, and would sit out front for hours, just trying to absorb all of it that he could.

Most of the family were a little skeptical of Gramp's tales; regarding the whole truth with some embellishments, but they were always interesting. As time went by, we found the same thing with June. There was always a little added, as she would say - to make it a little juicier or spicier. When he was a child in Warkworth, close to Banbury he used to go to school, and would put his cap in his back pocket. After roll call he'd cut out of the classroom for the rest of the day. When he was nine, the teacher told him "Well, Parrish, I've taught you all I know, I can't help you anymore". Gramp said then there was no point coming back – so he left school. He was well educated, but I don't believe he got much of it in school. He must have got it from reading. He had a talent for writing poetry.

Gramp fought in both the Boer War and the First World War. He never had any tales about the Boer War; he said it was best forgotten. There was one story he told however, over and over about the First World War, and it was always pretty much the same - so there was probably a lot of truth to it.

During the First World War, somewhere in Europe, there had been either a full battle or a skirmish the day before. He was never clear on that part of it. Anyway, there were still dead soldiers in the fields, which were being gathered up for burial. Otherwise the day was quiet. Gramp's friend, the cook,

George Parrish in his WWI uniform

had been able to acquire the ingredients to make ' spotted dick'. The cook got the pudding made and then needed a cloth to wrap it in, so he went off looking for one. After he found it, Gramp asked him where he got it from, but he wouldn't say. Later when the pudding was being served to the troops, Gramp asked the cook if he was going to have some. He said he didn't think he would. Gramp said; ' then I'm not either'. Much later, the cook told Gramp that; when he couldn't find a cloth, he found a dead Gerry, who was big and had a white undershirt on, so he took it off of him and used that. He figured that after it had been boiled in water, while being wrapped around the pudding for at least three hours, it would be clean enough. Gramp was always pleased he hadn't eaten any. The troops enjoyed it however!

Gramp was one to make you look at things and really see them. He always said he wasn't a religious man, but I don't think that was quite accurate. He used to say 'look at the trees', see how straight and tall they grow, and how the branches give a protective canopy for things to grow under them. Then he would take different leaves, and make you see the intricacies of their development. All the veins and different shapes. He would say; look at all these wondrous things, and then tell me there is no God, it is not possible. He said the scenery, especially the trees, were God's cathedral, and they were better than any built by man. The countryside was God's church, and that was all he ever needed.

He could not stand our local Vicar, Mr. Banham, who used to go past when Gramp was sitting out front of the house. As he went by, he would turn and say to Gramp; ' I will pray for you Mr. Parrish', and Gramp would always reply 'Don't bother, you have enough to do just praying for yourself'. Mr. Banham was most unpopular in the village, for many good reasons, so Gramp was probably right.

Gramp and June used to try and better the other in their stories. There was one in particular, where Gramp was saying he was digging in the garden, when a robin landed on the soil he had just turned over, and just stood there and sang to him. He said it was thanking him for exposing good things for it to eat. When June heard this, she said; 'Well, when I was digging, a robin landed on my shovel, and stayed there while I was digging'. Gramp called her a little rascal for saying such a fib.

One day, around Christmas time, he saw this old tramp walking past the house. He said it was bitterly cold, and he hoped he knew of a warm place to spend the night. He said, watching him trudge by, this poem came to his mind, and so he wrote it down. He later entered it in a competition in a London newspaper - it won a prize and it was printed in the paper.

THE OUTCAST

Christmas Night on a dark highway
A figure old, bent and gray
He was a social outcast
Stumbling along on the dark highway
And from the hill he heard the bells
Ring out so clear and bright
Telling the world a Christ was born
For it was Christmas Night

And he heard the childish trebles
In a street nearby
Singing that sweet old carol
"Glory Be to God on High"
He saw the cottage windows
With their tinsel coloured lights
And heard the laughter from within
And the shouts of childish glee
As they received their presents
From off the Christmas tree

The outcast stopped his thought
Went back to the time when he
Was like those children in their homes
And from all airs and care was free
And he thought of his dear old mother
Who had nursed him on her knee
And had taught him how to pray
And now he was a social outcast
Alone on the dark highway

He saw the village mansion
With lights on all aglow
And saw the merry couples
Dancing to and fro
They were a happy throng

And with a sigh of "Oh My God"
The outcast turned his head
And stumbled on
He passed the other cottages
Their lights they shone so bright
And on again to the dark highway
And the blackness of the night

And in the morn they found the outcast
Cold and still was he
His heart had ceased to beat
His soul was free
A smile was on his cold gray face
His hands clasped o'er his breast
For he had heard that soft voice
Calling "Come my son and outcast
Come with me and rest"
And it was Christmas Night.

Gramp used to write a lot of poems. He had apparently done this from a pretty young age, and when I was young he used to recite some to me. When I was about thirteen, I asked Gramp where they were, and he said he never kept them. I asked him to write down all he could remember and I would get them typed up. He seemed to like the idea of them being typed, so over a period of months I would get letters with a poem enclosed.

TRUTH
With the darkness comes the night
With the dawn, daylight
And so comes love and joy,
Peace, happiness
Hate, misery,
Jealousy and despair
And so it will be forever
For time has no end.
G.E.P.

This one was written for their fourth son, Walter, who died at the aged 17 of meningitis.

MEMORY

I sit alone by the fireside
Alone on a winter's night
And the memory of the past comes back
By the glow of its ruddy light

I sit and think of the day gone past
When all was oh so bright
And the children used to sing their hymns
By the fire on a winter's night

I sit and think of one so dear
Whose voice no more I'll hear
For he has gone to the Great Beyond
Where no one needs to fear

Walter Parrish 1932

And now I'm growing old and gray
As I sit by the fire tonight
But in my thoughts he will always be
God bless you all goodnight.
G.E.P.

The next one was written during the time Gran left Gramp, and went to London to live with one of their children for a while; I never got any more details than that. I was just told by Gran, that, that was in the past and isn't that important now.

PLEADING

Off times at night
From my sleep I awaken
Awaken my dearest thinking of thee
Often I fancy you hear my voice calling-

Come back my loved one
Oh come back to me
When down in the valley
To the green lane we wandered
We were so happy and all carefree
Alone in that green lane
My voice is now calling-
Come back my loved one
Oh come back to me

For I can never forget
Your dear sweet face
Your beautiful nut brown hair
Heed then oh thou my pleading
Heed then oh thou my prayer
Come back my loved one
Oh come back to me

Come back my loved one
I'm calling to thee.
G.E.P.

This one was written for their first grandchild, and my very special cousin Anthony (Tony), after he and his mother left Aynhoe, to live out the rest of the war in Wales with her family. He is the only child of Maurice and Gwen Parrish, Gran and Gramp's second son.

BUDDY

I shall always remember your smiling face
And your beautiful bright brown eyes
And I fancy I hear your laughter, Bud
And I fancy I hear you cry

Tony & Gwen
Parrish 1941

And now you have gone
From the old home
Where you were so happy to be
But I shall always remember little Bud
When I played with you on my knee

And I shall always remember
That sweet pretty smile
That made us so happy to see
It was that smile, little Bud
That captured the hearts
Of dear old Granny and me

And now in the eventide
I won't hear you cry
Or the voice of Mamie saying
"Dear be good"
But in my prayers each night
I will ask the great God
To bless my dear little Bud.
G.E.P.

Gramp had some routines, that he would not change with the modern era. When he got ready for bed, he would take his candle and candle holder out (the holder was like Jack be nimble's). He would light the candle, put two toffees in the saucer of the holder, take his hobnailed boots off, put his slippers on, and go upstairs to bed. He would not switch the electric light on; we all accepted it without comment. Until one day, June, in one of her devilment moods, ran over and switched the light on for him, he turned and said you little rascal; and switched it off. June loved to aggravate him that way.

He was known in the village, as someone you could set your clock by. If they were going past, and Gramp was outside beating the rugs they knew the time. Whatever he did, it was exactly the same every day. Dinner was at eleven thirty, and everything rotated around that.

He was a cabinet maker by trade. He made some nice pieces of furniture, a few pieces Mum still has, though most are gone now. One thing he made that always-fascinated June was a wooden roll up hot pad for putting hot pans on from the oven. It was made from slats of wood, about half inch square, and about fifteen inches long. These were joined together with flat braided cloth about an inch wide, woven under and over the slats at each end, so it could be rolled up when not in use. When you opened it up, if you did it fast and whipped it a bit it would make a loud cracking noise. That's what June really liked.

One thing very important to Gramp, was that everyone had clean shoes with a good shine on them. He said dirty shoes told you a lot about a person. My feeling was that it wasn't at all good, though he never specified. Every night we had to leave our shoes with Gramp, so he could have them clean for us to put on each morning. This included all the adults and children in the family. Each morning the shoes would be lined up in a row, sparkling clean, and he'd say; now isn't that some-thing to be proud of. We would all agree, and he would be proud his family was being sent out well shod.

There was a story about shoe cleaning when Mum was young. The boys had to take turns cleaning the shoes for everyone at night. This particular time, it was to be Walt's turn to clean the shoes that night. Mum was mad at Walt about something. So she made a special effort to have really dirty shoes for him to clean, even the laces were filthy. Later Mum was in the living room with Gran, helping with the mending. Walt came into the room and said to Gran, "Look Mam, do you think this is fair?" Gran asked whose they were. He told her they were Norah's. Gran looked very cross and told Walt – to not touch them, to take them back and leave them on the bench. Just before it was time for Mum to go to bed, Gran told her to go up into the wash-house, take a candle and clean her own shoes. Mum said, she would do it in the morning. Gran said "No, you will do it now." This made Mum re-ally mad, especially when she saw the smirking expression on Walt's face. Mum said she could have killed him. She really hated him at that time, and told him she wouldn't speak to him ever again. Walt said, "That's alright." Mum said she never pulled that trick again.

Gramp got up every morning at 4:30 am to do his chores. That was to clean the grate out, and re-light the fire for the days cooking, and for warmth in the winter. Once a week he would polish the grate with black lead polish. Then he would take the rugs out to shake and beat them, sweep the downstairs floors and put the rugs back down. Then he would polish all the shoes for the family. By then, it would be time to put the kettle on for Gran's morning cup of tea. He would take to her upstairs and wake her up. After she had had time to drink it, and get her thoughts together, he would bring up the jug of hot water for her to wash up with. When Gran got downstairs, everything was ready for her, as the table had been already been laid the night before. After breakfast, Gramp did the dishes, Gran dusted the living room, and then did whatever was destined for that particular day. Monday was wash day, Tuesday was ironing, Wednesday was to really clean the upstairs rooms, Thursday was downstairs, Friday was baking for the weekend, and Saturday was getting ready for Sunday. This way you only had to do bare essentials on Sunday, a day of rest and going for long walks as a family, usually dressed in your Sunday best.

Of course all the other things like gardening, allotments for home vegetables, building and fixing things were all fitted into these regular schedules. The only difference was that there wasn't the equipment or tools in those days to make jobs easier.

Aynhoe village women at King George V coronation celebrations 1910

Aynhoe village children and teacher at King George V Coronation Celebrations 1910

Married ladies egg and spoon race. Coronation celebrations 1910
Lt to Rt 3rd Mrs Ford, 4th Mrs Frank Garrett, 5th Mrs Williams
6th is Ada Parrish, 8th Mrs Judd, 10th Mrs Savings

1910 Flower show Aynhoe village men and boys

Lt to Rt Maurice, Ron, Alf, Ada &
Walt Parrish 1916

House at Station lt to Rt
Mrs Bowerman & Ron

Lt to Rt Adelaide Eaton,Ron,
Norah, Ada & Walt Parrish 1919

George & Denis Parrish 1925

Richard Cartwright's
21st Birthday decorations and
celebration.
Top Richard in front sitting cross
legged with all the male workers
at the Park ; Bill Wightman to
Richard's right.

Village decorations for George VI coronation: note Eaton's still has the 'E' for Edward in the window
Picture right: L-R Cherry West, Pocket Stayton., Den Parrish, Arthur Butler, John Eaton

Top lt; is Grape Harbour
Top rt: Lime Walk
Above : Summer House
The four others are part of the
gardens and Park land at the
Park house

Aynhoe villagers from 1920-40's

Opposite Page:

Top left:
Lt - Rt

Norah, Walter, Ada, Ronald, Denis Parrish, Adelaide & John Eaton

Top Right:
Lt - Rt

Frank, Ronald & Bernard Bowerman

Second Left:
Lt to Rt

The Parrish boys, Denis, Walter, Ronald, Maurice, Alfred

Third Left:

Charlie Wrighton the Station Masters family

Lt - Rt back row, Linda, Clarice, Vera
Lt - rt Front row, Madge, Edith and Charlie

Second Right:

Minnie (Wrighton) Greenaway and Mr Greenaway in front of their home up Brackley Road

Bottom Left:
Lt to Rt

Norah , Pat, Alf, Ada, George Parrish 1926

Bottom Right:
Lt to Rt,

Margaret Abernathy, Edna Watts, Beatie Butler, Grace Butler, Evelyn Butler, Joan Clements, Jean Abernathy, behind her is Doris Watts, Marge Butler, Dolly Smart, Norah Parrish, Kath Wilkins

Enough space is left for names to be written in by the reader if any are more people recognised:
Opposite Page
Top Left:

Aynhoe School students and teachers circa 1890's - Hopefully some of them will be recognised

Top Right:

May Day Festival 1913 May Queen is Gert Garrett .

Middle Left:

Aynhoe Infants 1910,
Lt -Rt on bench 3rd Gert Garrett , 5th is May Garrett

Bottom Right:

May Day at Aynhoe School 1914 hopefully some will be recognised

Bottom Left:

Circa 1915. A class believed to be of Souldern Children who were taught at Aynhoe school during this period

Top Left: c.1925

Lt-Rt top row, Will Garrett, Ron Smith, Ernie West, Ted Savings, Ron West, Bump Garrett. Lt-Rt middle row, Jim Brown, Ron Parrish, Ethel Watts, Mary Humphris, Lilian Bull (from station), Nell Hawkins, Mary Hawkins, Walt Upton, Walt Parrish,
Lt-Rt bottom row, Mabel Delahaunt (twin), Phil Page, Ivy Williams, Lilian Delahaunt (twin), Nancy Taylor, Maggie Horley

Top Right: c. 1925

Lt-Rt top row, Fred Horley, Les Jeacock, Reg Upton, Jim Smart, Les Ayres(Derb), Arthur Humphris, Nippy Ayres, Lt-Rt middle row, Joe Brown, Bill Butler (Bugseye), Jackie Garrett, Phil Upton, Norah Parrish, Margaret Meadows, Margaret Ford, Fred Smart. Lt-Rt bottom row, Beatie Hawkins, Beatie West, May Hawkins, Mary Garrett, Alice Williams, Gordon Lane, Tommy Humphris

Second down Left: c. 1930

Lt-Rt top row, Gordon Lane, Les Jeacock, Reg Upton, Arthur Butler, Fred Horley, Denis Parrish, Lt-Rt middle row, Doris Watts, Beatie West, Mary Greenaway, Joyce Nichols, Mary Upton, Teacher Miss Govier, Lt-Rt bottom row, John Eaton, Evelyn Butler, Joan Clements, unknown, Tommy Humphris, Joan Taylor.

Second down Right: c 1930 infants class.

Teacher Miss Sutton, Lt-Rt front row,Reg Greenaway, Brenda Williams, Joan Secal, Kath Wilkins, Mary Greenaway, Evelyn Butler, Fred Greenaway. Lt-Rt back row Fred Williams, Ted Secal, Ron West, Fred Butler

Third down Left: c. Mid 1930's

Front row Lt-Rt , 2nd Edna Watts, Dolly Williams, Doris Watts, B. Butler, Kath Wilkins, Grace Ayres. Back row 3rd from Lt John Eaton, teacher Miss Sutton

Third down Right c late 1920's

Teacher Miss Govier Front row L-R Glad Smart, Marg Butler, Joan Clements, unknown, Mary Greenaway. Middle row L-R Reg Greenaway, Milson Westbury, unknown, Joyce Nicholls, Brenda Williams, Charlie Williams, Back row L-R Fred West, Basil Humphries, John Humphries, L. Nicholls

Fourth down Left c 1945:

Back row Lt-Rt 4th Anne Shergold, Dawn Alsford, Neville West, Middle row 2nd from LT. Peter Thurgood`Front row Lt-Rt 1st Peddler Savings, 3rd June Alsford, 4th Pete Svenson, Pam Betts

Fourth down Right c. 1945:

Back row Lt-Rt 2nd Joan Garrett, Jean Garrett, 5th Valerie Bull. Front row 4th from lt. Dibby Wright, 6th Mick Garrett,

Bottom Left c. Early 1950's

Top row Lt-Rt Marion Garrett, unknown, unknown, Front row Lt-Rt Dibby Ayres, Joan Upton, Jill Parrish

Middle Bottom c. 1947 infants class, *Teacher Miss Govier.*

Top row Lt-Rt Nobby Ayres, John Belcher, unknown, unknown, unknown, Pete Shergold, unknown, unknown. Middle Row Lt-Rt Tony Ayres, George Ayres, far right unknown, Sitting Lt-Rt,June Alsford, Suzanne Parrish, Marion Garrett, ? Betts, Joan Garrett,
Christine Belcher, unknown ,Jennifer Garrett, Ground Lt-Rt. Pete Svenson,Peter Garrett, Unknown, David Belcher.

Bottom Right 1956:*Top row Lt-Rt Edwin Ayres, Ashley Grant, Pete Shergold, unknown, Bill Land, unknown, unknown. Front row Lt-Rt 3 unknown,, Nobby Ayres, Brian Garrett,*

Top Left: 1930 ish in front of the Church:
Back Row , Unknown, Miss Govier, Mr Cummins, Middle row, L-R Fred Greenaway, unknown, Loll Greenaway, Doll Smart, Kath Wilkins, Evelyn Butler, Fred West, Ron West, Lawrence Nicholls. Front row L-R Pink Savings, Blue Savings, Betty Greenaway, Basil Humphris, John Humphris, Grace Butler, Margery Butler.

Top Right, in vicarage gardens late 1920's:
Back row L-R 2nd Miss May, 5th Norah Parrish, Mr Banham, 11th Miss Ginger, Ada Brown.. Middle row on the rt. Holding her hands in front of her Joan Taylor, Front row, L-R 4th Les (Derb) Ayres,on his lap Tom Humphris, 6th Arthur Butler, 8th Denis Parrish, 11th Mary Greenaway.

Centre Left: *St Michael's and All Angels Church from Church path:*

Centre Right; *Walter Parrish on church path 1920's*

Bottom Church group 1920's

Top Left:
George and Alf Parrish sitting on a favourite spot the bank Station Road

Middle top:
Lt-Rt Ron and Bernard Bowerman up the Brackley Road

Top Right:
Top Miss May, Kneeling Lt-Rt Valerie Bull, Sybil Humphris, sitting, Lt-Rt, ,Anne Hovard, Joan Garrett, Suzanne Parrish, Jean Garrett, unknown

Centre Left:
The first seat down the Station Road, Lt -Rt Ada Parrish, Syd , Norman, June and Dawn Alsford 1946.

Centre Right:
Christmas Party in village Hall 1960's Back row L-R Gladys Mowatt, Evelyn Beasley,Sybil & Geoff Stevens, Ron Bowerman, Mr Ferris, unknown, George Watts, unknown. Middle row L-R unknown, Nell & Eric White, Rose Nicholls, Gladys Humphris, unknown, Mrs Weir, Molly Berry, Miss Spreckly, Barbara Ayres, Miss Watt, unknown, Lawrence Coles, unknown, Harry Humphris.

Bottom: *Christmas party for Companions Club 1950's*
Front row Lt-Rt Mrs Hetty West, Ben Hawkins, Mrs Hawkins, Miss Grey, Mrs Payne, Mrs Leonard Cross, Mr Stayton., Mrs Stayton., Mr and Mrs Westbury, Mrs Woolgrove, Jess Williams, Pudgy Williams
2nd row Lt-Rt unknown, Ralph Smith, Mrs Hunt, unknown, unknown, Olive and Lawrence Cole, Mr and Mrs Taylor, unknown John Howe, Lillian Dunn, Ada Parrish, Minnie Greenaway, Mrs Kirby, Mrs Butler, Mrs Lambert, Annie Smart.
3rd row Lt-Rt, Mrs Lewis, Mrs Wyeth, Nancy Shergold, Mr Lewis, Mrs Banham, unknown, Mrs Smith, Amy Ayres,
Back row Lt- Rt Col. Thompson, Mr Delahaunt,, Mr Smith, Chris Horley, Sid Upton, Cherry West, Charlie Shergold,

Celebrations in Aynhoe: *Top Left, Wedding reception at the village hall.*
Top right, a Coronation party in the village hall
Middle Left, and right , Children's Christmas performance 1970's at village hall
Bottom Left, Maypole dancing in school playground 1930's
Bottom right, Christmas party village hall 1970's

Aynhoe Villagers about mid- 1930's

Back row Lt-Rt men, Walt Upton, Charlie Upton, Harry Humphris, Unknown, Gordon Lane,

Included in the rest in no particular order is: *Gladys Smart, Ceenie Upton, Pink/Susan Savings, Gladys Nichols, Mrs Mowatt, Sybil Humphris, Jean Abernathy, Blue/Alice Savings, Betty Greenaway, Marjorie Butler, Joyce Nichols, Brenda Williams, Miss Annie May, a Braithewaite, Mrs Banham, Rev. Banham, Charlie Williams, Mrs Butler, holding Grace Butler, Gladys Humphris, Lizzie Upton, Sheila Upton, Miss Grey, Miss Ginger, Edna Watts, Christine Braithewaite, Margaret Abernathy, Kath Wilkins, Beatie Butler, a McClaren, a Braithewaite, Mrs Wilkins, Mrs Payne, John Humphris, Loll Nichols,, Evelyn Butler, Mary Greenaway, Doris West, Fred West, Fred Butler, Basil Humphris, Bob Oakey, Fred Greenaway*

Mrs Czeppe nee' Govier At Aynhoe School closing reception 1984

Chapter 10
End of the War and the Following Three Years

The excitement was felt throughout the village. The war was over and we had won. There wasn't going to be any more bombs dropped on us, and people wouldn't be killed by the Germans. We could have the lights on without the blackouts down. One day there would be lights in the towns again, and we would go there to see all the shops lit up. Of course, I had no idea what they were talking about, or why it was so special, as it obviously was to the grown-ups. There were to be great celebrations throughout the country, May 8th 1945 was VE Day.

I don't know if it was on the 8th that the big celebration was held in our village, but if it was they put it together at record speed. It was held in the Big Butts with all kind of things going on. All I can remember is, the Butts were full of people, and all kinds of stalls with activities at each. It was like a Fete or a fair with sideshows, all rolled into one. There is only one that I was totally fascinated with. This had two parallel poles held fairly high up by wooden upright posts. An army blanket was suspended across, and attached to each of the parallel poles, so the blanket hung down in the middle. Underneath the blanket was a very large trough of water. A person would get into the blanket and four people would hold the parallel poles at each corner and toss the person in the blanket until they ended up in the water. I don't know if there was any way to escape going into the water. It didn't make much difference, because that is where everyone ended up. This one had the most activity of all, and the biggest audience. A large part of the celebration, was seeing the planes used in the war, parked in the courtyard at the Cartwright Arms. Pilots were there to explain the controls to us and let us climb inside.

After the soldiers left the barracks at Aynhoe, there were loads of Nissan Huts that became empty. There were a lot of families without homes, and still living with their elderly parents or relatives, after being evacuated out of the towns. It was decided to convert these Nissan Huts into homes for them. Most were large enough to make two to four homes out of them, depending on how many bedrooms were needed.

After they were converted they were very pleasant inside. Generally the rooms were much larger than we were used to in our village cottages. Many of the children I played with in the village, moved into them, so I did get to see what several were like inside.

Other buildings at this time were used for things other than what they were intended for. One of those was the barn, that was across the main road at the bottom of the lane. After my father was de-mobbed he rented it to build furniture to sell, as he was a cabinetmaker by trade. Things definitely changed after Dad came home. There was a different feeling around home. Dad had been shell-shocked at the end of the war, so if there were any loud noises, such as a car back firing, and he was close by, he would black right out. He would just go straight down like a stick that fell. Sometimes he would grab your hand just before he went down. He would recover after a few minutes. There were also many disagreements between Mum and Dad. Mum used to say; she had made all the decisions when he was gone, now he was home he wanted to take over. I think Mum liked being the only one in charge and the one to make all the decisions, and now there was another person's input that had to be considered. I don't think she liked that situation at all anymore.

I'm not sure quite when, but Dad got a job at the Rehabilitation Hospital at Tusmore Park, as Chief Occupational Therapist. He was to teach cabinet making to the patients, so that they could earn a living after they were discharged. The patients all had head injuries, suffered while fighting in the war, and some also had spinal cord injuries. Tusmore was about five miles from home, and to get to it one had to travel on country roads. It was safe therefore for Dad to ride a bicycle there, without worrying about him blacking out. This seemed to make things better between Mum and Dad. After Dad had been working there for a while, he used to let me ride my bike and go with him to work. I liked that, as I found the patients and nurses interesting. Some of the patients had very severe disabilities. They couldn't move properly, and some couldn't talk, or they made strange sounds.

Gradually things improved after the war. Rationing was cut (except for sweets). Different things became available for us to buy in the shops. We had more freedom to run around as we got older, especially after we got our own bicycles. I got Uncle Walter's old bike. It was old fashioned with sit up and beg handlebars, but it gave me a lot more freedom.

As time went by, I was allowed to ride my bike pretty much anywhere I wanted. We liked to go to the canal, especially when they

were holding fishing competitions. There were always a lot of men entering it, and some were quite friendly. They would tell us how they were doing, and what type of bait they were using. I remember once, when we were down there, and Elizabeth Cartwright, the Squires daughter was with us. One of the fishermen was using maggots, and they were all wriggling around look-

Fishing group at the canal: Far Rt standing George Parrish , sitting Charlie Wrighton

ing horrible. They fascinated Elizabeth, so the man gave her some, and she put them in her pocket. Her governess, Miss Young, who was with us, was not too pleased about it when she showed them to her, but she wouldn't give them up.

Another great favourite of ours was in the spring, to ride over to Newbottle Woods on the other side of Charlton. Under the trees grew thousands of primroses. It used to look like a yellow carpet as far as you could see. We would pick the flowers and tie them into small posies, with their leaves around the edges to protect the blooms. We used one long piece of yarn, so it looked like a chain of posies, and we would tie them to our handlebars. They looked very pretty. When we got back to the village, we would give a posy to each of the elderly people in the village, especially the ones at the Alms Houses, being sure to save enough for our own families.

It wasn't long after the war, that they replaced all the cobblestone paths in the village with stone slabs. They were not laid at all uniform like they are now. They were more like a crazy paving, only cemented in place. It was

Aynhoe before the cobble stone paths were removed

129

definitely easier on your feet, because our cobblestones weren't the little round ones, but more like small bricks, not cemented in place and terrible for bike riding.

The other big events that started up were the Flower Shows, at the Park House, and the garden shows for people to win prizes for best vegetables or flowers grown. The best sewing, knitting, preserving or baking competitions were included. There were events for all to enter, even the children. That is where I won a hand sewing second prize, and a prize for a wild flower collection one year.

There was apple bobbing, that was fun, -apples suspended on a string, trying to get them in your mouth with your hands behind your back. The races were, egg and spoon, sack, three legged and wheelbarrow races. You don't use a wheelbarrow for that, rather one person is the wheelbarrow, and the other pushes them along holding their legs up. There was folk dancing, bonnie baby competitions, and knobbly knee competitions for the men. The Fetes lasted all day and were lots of fun.

Aynhoe sports day in 1950's

As I got older, I found out about jigsaw puzzles and became a big fan of them. My parents just couldn't afford to keep me supplied in them, so I would do the same ones over and over again. I was doing 500- 750 piece puzzles. In my travels amongst the older people in the village, and my preference for the company of older people, I met a lady who liked puzzles as much as I did. Her name was Miss Savage, who lived at Rose Cottage. She also liked to garden ,and I used to help her weed. Whilst we were weeding, we got talking about puzzles, and she said she had lots and that we should swap. If she had one of mine, and I had one of hers, we would each get a change. When we had finished with, them we swapped back. I liked this idea - the only problem was, that I ran out of puzzles to swap, long before she did. She would just say she would like to do one of mine again, because she really liked it. I did realise she was just being very kind to me.

In July 1947 Gran took me to London for a week. We were going to stay with Gwen, Maurice and my cousin Tony, at their flat in Croydon. Tony had been down and stayed with Gran in Aynhoe a few times since the war, and we had become more like a brother and sister that actually got along. We did loads of exploring around Aynhoe, and had much the same interests. Therefore I was really looking forward to going, plus I would have Gran pretty much to myself.

Their flat was on the top floor of a very large house. The kitchen was huge, with a dining table in the middle and running water to the kitchen sink. We seemed to spend most of our time there. There was also a living room with a fancy dining room table in it. I believe there were three bedrooms and a bathroom. It was all very light and airy. The back garden was very large and enclosed, so it was safe for children to play out there on their own.

We did not spend a lot of time there, because Gran wanted me to see the London sights. We went to the Tower of London and saw the Crown Jewels. They were housed in the little tower called The Wakefield Tower, so there wasn't room for all of them to be on display. One piece that caught my eye was a salt cellar, which was large enough to be a play castle instead of a playhouse for a child. I couldn't imagine having something that large on the dinner table just for salt. We saw where people got their heads cut off, the bedroom where the two Princes were murdered, and the steps to where their bodies were found a hundred or more years later. There was the walk, where Sir Walter Raleigh got his exercise before he was eventually beheaded. Additionally there was the wall where the heads were displayed on stakes, for all to see after the deed was done. We stopped to see Tower Bridge and the River Thames before we left the area.

We saw Buckingham Palace, the Mall, and walked through St James Park to Big Ben and the Houses of Parliament. We got to go inside Westminster Abbey to see where the Throne was that was used for the coronations. The pillars inside are so huge all around, and so high they looked like trees. The windows were all stained glass, that I remembered were so beautiful. What I thought was strange was, that there weren't any church pews in there for people to sit on. Instead they just had chairs all lined up in rows - to me it looked untidy. We went to see Piccadilly Circus with the Eros statue in the middle.

I believe that day we also went to see Madame Tussaud's, which is probably the most famous wax museum in the world. All of the statues were so lifelike, it was almost impossible to tell them from a real person. At that time it was arranged like a house, with many rooms in it. As you travelled from one room to the next, there were displays of all kinds. There would be a group of the Royal family or the current politicians. Then there would be famous celebrities, or well known stories depicted. One that I liked was of Sleeping Beauty, lying in her coffin, and they made her so she looked like she was breathing. There was a Chamber of Horrors. This apparently showed gangsters, murderers, etc. in their cells or being tortured. I chose not to go down there! One entered and left the building the same way, through a very large entrance hall that had a sweeping staircase, at the bottom of which stood a policeman in his Bobby's uniform. He looked very real. It was fun to stand in the hall and watch the people go up to him and ask directions to different things. Then to see the look on their faces, when they realised they were talking to a dummy.

1947 Dawn at Trafal-
gar Sq w Gran far rt.

The other place, that was at the top of my list of the most fun things we did, was to go to Trafalgar Square, feed the pigeons and climb on the big lion statues. The pigeons were the best part of it. We would buy small cups of grain from one of the vendors, put some into your cupped hands, and then hold your arms out straight. The pigeons would land on your hands and eat the grain, others would land on your head, shoulders or anywhere they could get a hold, waiting to get their chance at the food in your hand. There were photographers around, who would take your picture that you could buy, and they would mail them to your home after they were developed. I still have mine.

It was so much fun all week, I didn't want to go back home. I enjoyed spending this time alone with Gran. It was around this time that I said to Gran; that I couldn't wait to be a Grandmother like her. She told me I had to be a mother first, before I could be a grandmother. That did not impress me too much, as I really wanted to figure out a way to skip that step in the process.

During 1947, Infantile Paralysis (Polio) was raging throughout the country, with the greatest fear for all parents being, that their child would be struck down with it. There were horror stories of children, and young adults, having to spend the rest of their lives in an iron lung. We were kept away from places that were considered danger spots, and if a child needed their tonsils out, it was delayed until late autumn for this to be done. If they had their tonsils out during the Infantile Paralysis season, they were found to be at greater risk of getting it. Because of this, once the risk had passed, there were hundreds of children needing their tonsils out, so the hospitals used to have what they called 'tonsil drives'. I was lucky or unlucky enough to be in one of them.

It was November 7th 1947, the day I was to have my tonsils out at the Radcliffe Infirmary in Oxford. For my parents this meant a train ride from Aynhoe to Oxford to take me there. We arrived about 10.00 am in this large ward that seemed to have one large room and several smaller rooms. The smaller rooms had about four beds in each. The large room had many more, plus children's size tables and chairs in the middle.

By the middle of the afternoon, all the beds were full of children of all ages. There must have been at least 30 of us. Most were just playing together after all the parents had left. I do not remember anyone telling us what was going to happen to us. About 5pm they brought in a stretcher and started putting three to four children, sitting up on each one, depending on the size of the children, and told us we were going for a ride. I was not put on a stretcher, instead someone came and picked me up, and said he was going to carry me down there. We were going to lead the way. This was because my last name was Alsford, and that began with an "A", so I was going to be special and first for everything. Lucky me! They took us to this room,and sat us all down on the floor around the wall. I was closest to a door at the end of the room. The man that carried me down started to entertain us all, even while they gave each one of us an injection.

After a while someone picked me up and carried me into another room, and laid me down on this narrow table with a sheet on it. There were about three people, standing over by what looked like a fireplace, and the room was all painted green. One of the people came over, and told me he was going to put something over my face, and it would smell funny and I would then fall asleep. When I woke up, my tonsils and adenoids would be all gone, and then tomorrow I would go home. The last thing I remember was a horrible smell.

When I woke up, I was in bed. It was dark but for a single light in the large room. I could hear someone crying, and a nurse talking quietly to her. Once my eyes got used to the light, I noticed my pillow was all red. I got very scared because I thought it was all blood. I called for a nurse; she came over and explained it was just a red cover over the pillowcase. She gave me just a sip of water, then I realised how sore my throat was. She told me it would soon feel a lot better.

Early the next morning they got us all up, and we were shuffled off to the bathrooms. When we came back, our beds were all stripped, and the tables were set with our breakfasts. It was porridge. None of us wanted to eat, as our throats hurt too much. We were told we were all going to be taken home in ambulances, as soon as we had eaten our breakfasts, but if we didn't eat it all up, we wouldn't get to go home. We all ate it, but not without a few tears. Then we were moved into what was like a storage room, with mattresses all over the place. We just sat on them and waited. After a while someone came in, and organised us into different ambulances to take us home. There were about 12 children in my ambulance. As we left the room, we saw more children coming into the place we had been. It was now their turn.

It took the best part of the day to deliver us to the different villages. Mine was one of the last ones. My name beginning with "A" didn't mean too much anymore. Those were the "Tonsil Drives", until they got the immunisation against Infantile Paralysis, or Polio as it is called now.

The winter of 1947-48 was one to go down in history, or in the record books, as one of the worst winters ever. It was not long after Christmas and it had become very cold. We woke up one morning, and found we could not get out of the house, because the snow was so deep. It took over a week before a narrow path was cut through to the school. The problem was, that the snow just kept coming. People were running out of food and water. I don't remember, how long it took to get food through to the village, but it was like being back in the war. When they cut the path to the school, my sister and I went up there to find there

134

was only one other child in the school besides us. It took a while before all the children could get back in school.

There was no fun attached to this snow. It was too deep and too dangerous to go out and play in it. In any case, all we had was metal trays to sit on and use as sledges, and we couldn't get anywhere to use them. That winter was very long, and very hard on the whole country. The summer that followed was glorious; it was hot and sunny almost all summer. Then they were concerned about the drought. It was agreed by all, that it certainly made up for the winter.

By this time, the thing that concerned Anne Shergold and I, was that she was going to be nine on July 15th - St Swithin's Day or Apple Christening Day. We both agreed that was a great age to be, and we weren't too sure we were ready for it yet. At least I had to wait till February. My problem, we decided, was even greater, because the way my parents had been talking, it looked as if we would have moved to Oxford by then. Tusmore Park was going back to the owners to use as their home, and the Hospital was moving to an estate on the outskirts of Oxford. They wanted Dad to go as well, and there was a house on the grounds they wanted us to live in, so he would be nearer for the patient's needs. Mum and Dad had been to see the house and really liked it. They said it was large, and had indoor plumbing. There was work to be done on it, but I could have my own bedroom. I think they were telling me this, because I was so upset about leaving the village and my grandparents. I was also going to be that dreaded nine and away from home. Things were not so much fun for me at home anymore. It seemed as if I had lots of chores to do every day.

During this time, I used to spend all the time I possibly could, down home at Gran & Gramp's. They were my lifelines where everything was just right. They said things would be better, when Mum no longer had the worry of moving, and we were settled in Oxford. My fear was, when I was in Oxford, I would not have Gran & Gramp to escape to. I had asked if I could stay with them, but Mum wouldn't let me. She said I belonged with them, and in any case I was just beginning to be useful around the house. I dreaded the move so much, and it came the day after Boxing Day - December 27th 1948. It was sunny, I was not, and I was going to be the dreaded nine years old in February!

Chapter 11
The Woods

The move to Oxford was all the things I dreaded – isolation, no friends, and strange schools where teachers ridiculed me for being a country kid. The house, or Lower Lodge as it was called, was originally the gate-house for the Morrells estate. The own-er of the Oxford brewery's home, was now the hospital for the patients receiv-ing rehabilitation. The main house, that sat at the top of the hill, was known as Headington Hill Hall, or HHH. This was where the rehab hospital was to be housed, and it kept the name. This is also where all the patients and nurses lived, and the offices were located.

Headington Hill Hall Rehabilita-tion Hospital 1948 - 1959

Part of the original estate, was a dairy with a house attached. This was located half way up the hill on the main road. A former em-ployee of Morrells still lived there, but the dairy hadn't been operational since before the war. There were lots of good places to hide around there. The trees had grown up very closely around the buildings. In ad-dition there were two huge walnut trees in front of the dairy, which pro-duced a lot of nuts each year. We used to gather them when they were still in the green casing. Mum would turn them into pickled walnuts. She used to get the large glass sweet jars from the sweet shop, the kind they kept the hard sweets in, and fill two of them with the walnuts. They weren't ready to eat until they had turned black. Then one could cut through them with just a fork, even though the hard green casing was never removed. Now it costs a fortune just to have a small jar of them.

At the top and the bottom of the hill, on the main road in the grounds, was a gate lodge. These lodges were homes for the Morrells gatekeepers to live in. The occupants were responsible for opening the large wrought iron gates, for carriages or people to pass through. They were about ten feet high and very heavy. There were of course no more carriages, and if anyone wanted the gate open, they opened it themselves. We lived in the one at the bottom of the hill.

There was a wide driveway, that went from the gates in front of our house, up to the main house. It had an avenue of Horse Chestnut trees, that edged the driveway all the way to the main house. They all had white blooms in the spring, except the two in front of our

Lower Lodge 1950

house, and those blooms were red. In the spring the driveway looked beautiful. In the autumn it was great because we had the 'mother load' of conkers for our conker matches.

These chestnut trees had been allowed to grow, so the lower branches curved down towards the ground. This meant that some of them were no more than three to four feet off the ground. This gave us excellent access to the trunks. These lower branches were about 18 inches thick, making it possible to walk up them to the trunk. Then the rest of the branches were close enough, so we could almost run up to the tops of the trees and down again. Hilary Barber and I used to compete with each other. She was a friend I had met at school, who lived the closest to us, in the Magdalen College Sports Ground. We would start on either side of the path, and climb as far as we could up each tree, to Mr. Stockfords path, then cross over and come down the other side. Some of the trees were pretty tough to negotiate, so we didn't get far up those. Once, during one of these competitions Hilary found 16 Mars Bars neatly stacked on top of one of the branches, four or five of us ate them very quickly. Only recently we found out; Hilary's husband Brian Mullins had put them there. When he went to get them, they were all gone. Now he knows why!

We had one particular tree which we both considered our favourite. We carved our initials up at the top when we were about ten years old. We were able go up and down that one as if we were squirrels, until we were 16 years old. About a year before that, Mum had told us we were to stop climbing, as it wasn't lady like.

I was home from nursing school and Hilary had come over. We were reminiscing about our tree, and wondering if our initials could still be seen up there. We decided we should check it out one last time, just for old time's sake. We got to the top just fine and of course our initials were still readable. When we decided we had better get down, before Mum came home. We found we couldn't. Somehow it all seemed to be different. We were hoping Norman would come home from school before Mum did, but we weren't so lucky. When she spotted us, she told us we deserved to spend the night up there. It was some time after Norman came home, that she let him come and help us down. We were beginning to think she meant it.

Our house was 'L' shaped, with four windows in each room. It was built that way, so that no matter what room you were in, you could see the gate, or see if someone was approaching. That way, the Morrells would not have to wait too long, for the gate to be opened for them. Each leg of the 'L', had a large room up and down in it, and at the joint part of the long leg, there was a single bedroom upstairs (my room), and the bathroom. Underneath it was the kitchen, a back porch and an outside toilet. There was a large garden all around the house. Both my parents worked hard in the garden, and they really got it looking very nice, with lots of flowers, shrubs and, of course, vegetables. One of my jobs was to weed it all.

Around the perimeter of the whole property, were woods with trees that were not much good for climbing. They were all pretty well overgrown and spooky, so we decided that they were haunted. The Bottom woods ran along Marston Road, and were separated from the road by a stone wall, up to Mr. Stockfords bungalow. St Clements Church and Church Yard were across the road, so we decided the woods were definitely haunted!

This wall was where the kids from St Clement climbed over, to get into the woods to play. The grounds were supposed to have been private. So our friends and we used to have a lookout club, to watch for these other kids sneaking over. We had endless places to hide, from hollowed out trees, to brush and tops of trees. We had a signal that told us if we spotted them, and other signals to tell us where they were. Then we would encircle them, gathering clumps of soil from the huge anthills that were everywhere. When we had a good advantage, we would charge them, throwing the clumps of soil with the ants in it, at their necks. They'd take off running and we would stand back and laugh at them. We were such nice children!

Mr. Stockford was the gamekeeper for the Morrells, and he was allowed to stay on living in his bungalow as long as he wished. He still found some game to shoot. He used to bring Mum half a dozen pigeons every now and again, for her to make a pie. She used to thank him and then throw them away or bury them. She said they were too small and fiddly, to be worth the effort of plucking and cleaning them. She didn't want to hurt his feelings, so she never let him know what she did. He was a nice old man and very kind to us kids. The path that led to his bungalow, also led to the gate that we went through, to cross the road to go to Hilary's home.

The area in the centre of the grounds was the best part, as there were open areas, but with the occasional large tree in it. In this part, at one time, they must have planted a very large raspberry and blackberry patch. They were definitely cultivated, because of the size of the fruit. They were at least three times larger than the wild ones. In season we used to gather all the fruit, and Mum would make jam or jelly out of it. We would also have pies, and anything else Mum could think of to use them up. Hilary used to take a lot home for her family, and we would take a lot up to the hospital, for the cooks to use for everyone there. These berry patches were huge and very productive, so we were able to have plenty of jam each year.

The other thing that grew wild, along the main driveway, was strawberries. There were the usual small red ones, but there was another kind that never turned red, but stayed a beautiful creamy colour. They were about three times larger than the red ones, and very sweet tasting. I have never seen any like them since. Mum would mix the red and cream ones together and make jam out of them. They would often maintain streaks of lighter colour in the jam even after the cooking. It was very good.

My parents used to keep chickens for eggs, and cockerels to be fattened up for Christmas. The ones we didn't eat, they would sell to get the new ones for the next year, and enough to pay for their feed for the year. Between all that, and what there was on the property, we were able to get a decent amount of food out of it. It would have been even better if there had been such a thing as a freezer available to the home owner back then.

Sometimes our cousin Tony, would come down from London to stay with us for a week. During those times, I didn't have quite so many jobs to do, so we were able to spend some time together exploring and the like. This one time we were gathering some wood for the fire. Generally we would just get fallen wood. Occasionally we would spot a dead branch and would just break it off of the tree. It was easy to do. You just to get a good grip on it, start it swinging back and forth, then give it a good hard pull towards you, and it would snap off up by the trunk, so none was wasted.

I spotted this particularly good looking branch. It was hanging down, but to reach it, to get the grip I needed on it, I had to jump up, grab it and get it underneath my body, to be able to start swinging it. Well I did this just fine, except it wasn't quite as dead as it looked. I lost my grip on it, and it came up and hit me in the face twice, before I was able to get out of its way. The blood flowed like crazy, and my nose was a mess. Tony grabbed me and helped me run home, leaving a considerable trail of blood. When we got home, Mum said I had just broken my nose, made me lie down and put a wet cloth on my face. My face swelled up, and I had two awful black eyes. It took a long time for the swelling to go down. When it did, I was left with a nose that didn't work well in the breathing department. It looked like the River Nile from the front and Dick Tracy's from the side. Plus it was twice the size of what it was before.

From that time on, if I had a cold, breathing was extremely difficult. Kids in school would make fun of my large crooked nose. Because I did my growing early, I was the tallest kid in the school and other kids would look up at me and say; "'ain't you got a big nose". I reached the point, that when I was around other people, I would cover my nose up to try and hide it. As an adult I would hear people say, "You know, Dawn would be pretty good looking if it wasn't for that nose". This is a very good way to get an inferiority complex.

Years later, after my nose had been fixed to make it look better, (not that it functioned any better), I broke it again. Because it happened at work they insisted on X-raying it. They said to me, "You have had extensive trauma to your face in the past haven't you?" I told them

I had fractured my nose a few times, and had surgery on my nose to make it look better. So they told me to come and take a look at the X-ray. They said it was a very old injury, because of the extent of the calcification. What they showed me, explained the reason for my problems throughout the years. It showed that when the main injury had happened, I had fractured all my sinuses and my face, to the extent that the front of my face could have been lifted out in the shape of a saucer. They asked me what treatment I had received for it. I told them my mother put a wet wash cloth on it for a few hours.

After seeing the extent of the injury, I finally understood the reason for the amount of pain I had suffered, and why it hurt so much even years later, whenever my face, especially my nose was hit or even just bumped. It also explained why my nose doesn't function too well.

Chapter 12
Headington Hill Hall

There was a back path, which was a shorter walk to the hospital from our house, that went past the dairy. Along the path there was a patch of clover, which only produced four leaf clovers instead of the usual three. Just before one came to the lowest level of the gardens surrounding the hospital, there was a steep bank. In the spring this bank was covered with daffodils for as far as you could see. It was really beautiful.

One year, Hilary and the three of us, thought we would pick some daffodils for our mothers. The only trouble was, they were still in straight up buds, so we could hold a lot without realizing how many we had. In a very short time we had filled our arms to capacity. When we arrived home, so proud of what we had gathered, we expected the same response from Mum. We were surprised when she was less than happy, though she could see the humour in it.

She was concerned that Dad would get into trouble again, for something we had done. We told her we didn't gather them all in one area. There were still plenty of daffodils left. She hoped they wouldn't notice - they didn't. Mum found every available container she could think of to put them in, from buckets, jars, jugs and vases. Not counting the armful Hilary took home to her Mother. Mum had at least three vases full of daffodils on each windowsill. The buckets and jugs held the ones that were still in very tight buds, and those she just put on the floor in the dining room, because it was the coolest room in the house. As the daffodils died in the vases, she replenished them with the ones from the dining room. Our house was very "spring" like for a long time. Mum told us it was a nice thought, but we were not to do it again.

Just past the daffodil bank, the garden to the main house had three levels - all beautifully landscaped with flowerbeds and shrubs. Some were very large and had flowering trees. There were even specimen trees, such as Monkey trees.

The gardener used to like to put love-lies-bleeding plants, along the front of the flowerbeds. They have blooms that are about an inch thick, about ten inches long, and hang down like a tail. One year June and Norman went down the whole bed, and tied them all together in knots. The gardener was not amused, and they had to go back and untie them all. That was not so easy without tearing them.

To the right of the short cut path, was a path that circled the lower garden. There was a large part of the lawn, that had what we called a putting green, but it wasn't like putting greens as we know them today. It was more like a real golf course, but confined to an area of about 300 square feet. The green had ten holes, and in each hole there were poles with flags on them. We used a golf ball and a golf club to play. As many people as you want can play at once. We played it a lot by ourselves, or with the patients at the hospital. They were commonly known as the boys rather than patients. In the lower corner of the putting green, was a tulip magnolia. It was about fifty feet in diameter, and in the spring, when it was in full bloom, it looked like a massive half ball of white and pink. The perfume from it was amazing.

On the top level was the hospital, a three-story building, square shaped and built entirely of stone. The house was typical of most large stately homes found all over England. The interior had not been changed from the original construction. Only the use had changed. The ground floor held two large wards for some of the boys, and the rest were dining rooms for staff, with another room for the boys and a very large kitchen. What used to be the ballroom, with pocket doors between the rooms, still had the pocket doors, but one side was the TV room, and the other was the games room. The first floor rooms were either large wards for the boys, or offices for Matron and another for a doctor. The physical therapy room and a sewing room were also located there. The Red Cross ran the hospital, so one of the larger rooms served as the office of Miss Tomlinson, the Commandant. The top level, the former servant's quarters, was where the nurses lived, and Matron, the head of the nurses, had her apartment. They were nice sized rooms and very bright and cheerful.

We spent a lot of time in the boys' dining room, especially Norman. He used to like to help them with their eating. We were taught not to actually do anything for them, rather to help them accomplish what they were trying to relearn, as this was what rehab was all about. This one fellow was a particular favourite of everyone. His name was Dennis Dunn. He had been buried alive at Dunkirk, for 12 days before he was found. He was 18 years old at the time. When he was first brought to Stoke Mandeville Hospital, which was the central rehab hospital for the whole country, he was on a stretcher and could neither sit nor stand, and he certainly could not feed himself. By the time he came to our rehab hospital he was a little better; he was in a wheelchair but could not feed himself.

He had no perception as to where his mouth was, so a person would sit in front of him, and tell him which way to go with his fork or spoon to hit his mouth. Norman used to love to help him with this. The only trouble was the two of them would get to laughing so much, that his misses got wild. They would generally end up in his ear. By this time he was doing pretty well with talking, but it was with his mouth open wide, causing his voice to sound hollow and loud.

His closest friend was Georgie Walsh. To look at him he did not look as if he had any injuries, though Dad said his head injury was one of the worse. He could talk and walk fine, and do most gross functional things. But he couldn't read or write, or process any of the fine motor things we need for normal functioning.

Dennis and Georgie were inseparable. When Dennis finally learned to walk, with 2 sticks stuck out as far as he could laterally get them, his main goal was to walk down the short path to our house for a cup of tea. When this memorable day arrived, I was in the garden weeding, and here came the two of them laughing like crazy. I said: "Dennis you're fantastic, you've made it. Did you fall many times?" He said "Only fifty six." They got their tea. Needless to say this was the first of many trips.

A newer electric wheelchair, but similar to what we used

There were several boys that were paraplegics, and besides the standard wheelchairs, they also had electric ones for going longer distances. These were nothing like a regular wheelchair. The seat was situated at the back between 2 large wheels. The 3rd wheel was about 4-foot front of them. There was a board between the seat and the front wheel, and then there was a waterproof apron that came from the front, to fit around the waist of the person riding in it.

Dennis had one of these, and Georgie would borrow one from someone else. Jimmy Brennan, another paraplegic, would bring his as well, and the three of them would come down to our place, especially when they knew Mum and Dad were gone. Then we would line them up abreast across the driveway, we kids would sit on the board part in front, and we would have races.

People with head injuries, frequently have no depth perception, and have field cuts, so they may not see anything in part of their field of vision. Their physical function is often limited, and to say the least, incapable of keeping anything in a straight line. To this, add three men, plus three kids laughing egging them on and trying to win a race, knowing all the time we really shouldn't be doing what we intended to do. Crashes were inevitable, if not guaranteed. We always ended up in a pile, either in the driveway or on the grass verge, laughing so much that we were incapable of getting the boys, or ourselves up, until we had laughed ourselves out. Then trying to untangle the mess, and lift the boy's back into the chairs, was something else to behold. The reality of the situation was, these were grown men and we were just kids. Their dead weight made lifting a problem.

The staff at the hospital, and our parents did not know half the antics we got into, but they all said we were the best thing for the boys, because everything they did with us, they just saw as fun, not a part of any learning process. Of course they learned a lot, as did we. Eventually we grew too big to continue doing this, and it wasn't as much fun if there was no one riding in the front.

Learning to play games, such as table tennis, billiards, golf on the putting green, even cards and doing puzzles, with people who have had head injuries, is a whole new experience. A lot of head injuries, cause a person to lose the use of either side of their body. In other words, they are paralysed on the right or the left, meaning they have no use of their right or left arm and leg. They usually put a brace on the affected leg, to help them to walk by giving them some stability. The arm usually just hangs at the side. To learn to play these games with these limitations, or from a wheelchair because they are paralysed from the waist down, is a challenge. It is also a challenge to play the games with them. One has to play with consideration for their blind sides, and the fact that a sudden movement can cause them to go off balance. This could be taking unfair advantage of them. As time went by, and they became more skilled, then it was fair and fun to challenge them to do even more. We never let them just win a game, but sometimes we would put a hand in our pockets to even it up a bit. As I got older and knew how to play tennis, there were a couple of the boys with hemiple-

gia, who used to like to have a match with me. There was a tennis court, up on the level above the hospital in the grounds.

Wheel chair pt. Using lathe with use of only 1 arm

In addition to the tennis court on that level of the grounds, there were the three workshops. One was run by the women occupational therapists. They taught weaving, the making of lampshades, leather work and basket weaving, to the boys that wanted that for an occupation when they went home. The other work-

shops were where Dad worked. He taught all types of woodworking, from furniture making to wood turning on lathes, and carpentry. Then, in a back room, there was one section that was heat controlled, where he taught French polishing.

He devised or adjusted power tools and equipment, so they could be operated by a person from a wheelchair, or for a person with only one working arm and hand. He also taught me how to use most of them. He was very big on the three of us learning how to do most of the crafts that were taught there. We were able to make all kinds of gifts for friends and family members, for Christmas and birthdays.

Early prototype of the lift/ hoist

Dad invented the first lift for getting patients out of wheelchairs into a bed, or into bathtubs and into and out of cars. It was called the Oxford Lift, and he was so busy getting it into production with a friend of his, and into the houses of patients that had already gone home, that he failed to get it patented, so he lost out on

146

any financial rewards – the 'friend', patented it instead. The same type of lift is now used everywhere.

The first one he built was made entirely of wood, and was attached to a bed. He had built the bed so large, to counter the weight of the person, it would have never fitted inside a normal sized house. By this time I was about 13 or 14 years old, and, as it turned out, fully-grown, so he used me as the patient. This way none of the patients, or employees, was put at risk if it collapsed. I guess he thought I could move quicker than the others could if it did. Eventually it was made of some form of metal or steel on wheels, and was very manageable for just one person to use, which was the whole idea behind it. The swing seat was made out of a new material called nylon, which Mrs. Barber (Hilary's Mother) told Dad about; she thought it would be strong enough to hold the heaviest person. That same material is still used for it today.

Dad & Dr Ritchie-Russell using hoist for dual lift. Plus slings Mrs Barber recommended

Our lives really revolved around the hospital, the boys and their activities. Whether it was pleasure boat rides on the River Thames, or taking them swimming in the River Cherwell, we went along. We were able to help the staff getting them into, or onto, whatever means of conveyance was used for whatever they were doing. We enjoyed it too. The swimming was especially amazing. If the patient could swim before their injury, and wanted to go, they went, no matter what the extent of their injury.

What was really fascinating, was to watch a person with paraplegia crawl out of his wheelchair, and slither across the ground pulling his legs behind him, slide into the river, and then swim as if he had the full use of his legs. It was explained to me that the reason they can do this, is because of the buoyancy that the water affords them. The boys loved to there; they said that it made them feel normal while they were swimming.

Every year, Stoke Mandeville Hospital held a sports day for all their former patients, which actually lasted two days. Most of them were still in rehab, at one of the satellite rehab hospitals like ours. We always went with them to help with the boys. It was all very competitive, with all kinds of competitions to enter.

My favourites were the wheelchair basketball games. They got very rough, with bodies flying everywhere. These were played as elimination matches, until the team that won the most games was the overall winner. The other one that I liked was the wheelchair archery. This was done in teams, and had several rounds until the winning team was declared. I guess it was the forerunner to the Paralympics, except these were all adults.

Each of the boys had their own special needs and personalities. Most of them, because of their head injuries, were susceptible to having seizures. We all had special type tongue depressors, with a thick rubber band around them. These were used if a patient had a seizure when we were with them. We could put it in their mouths to protect them from biting their tongues.

There was one patient named Charlie. We had been told, if we were with him and that he started to have a seizure, we were not to help him. We had to get away from him as fast as we could, and to run for help. The reason for this was, that he was very strong, and when he went into a seizure, he tended to grab for something with his two hands and then bend it. They said that; if he got a hold of one of our arms, he would snap it in two.

There was another patient named Barney, who before the war had been a maths college professor. His injury had left him unable to read or write, but if a problem was read to him, he could work it out in his head, and tell you how to write it down. He helped me a lot with my homework.

Bob Morley was a preacher's son and he had been a very quiet, studious person prior to his injury. He had been left with the need to constantly tell dirty jokes, and to swear with every other word he spoke. When with him, you could not be judgmental, but just keep telling him that is not the proper thing to say in company. I don't know if he ever improved.

Smokey was one who had to have a mission in life. His mission was to come down to our house everyday at 1 o'clock, to make a pot of tea, and to serve it to everyone including a bowl full for the dog. If when he arrived, we were still eating dinner, he would grunt, give us all a disgusted look, push past us and go ahead making the tea. He would only let my mother wash and cut his hair. Mum really hated doing it, because he had so many deep pits in his skull, from all the surgeries he had undergone. Mum would try and skim over them, but he would tell her to dig into them. She said it really turned her stomach over. He ended up marrying one of the occupational therapists, and moving to Australia.

Wooden pot Jimmy Brennan turned and gave me one Christmas

From the time we moved to Oxford, we never spent Christmas Day at home. The Boys wanted us to spend it with them, and they wanted us to open our gifts from Father Christmas in front of them. So, what we did every year was, very carefully open our gifts, then re-wrap them to take them up to the hospital.

They had a large Christmas tree in the entrance hall, which was about fifty feet square. The Boys and staff would gather around, and some would sit on the large sweeping staircase, to watch us open our gifts. We had to act surprised, and take our time doing it, so it didn't get confusing for them. They would have gifts for us, usually things they had made. I still have one that Jimmy Brennan made for me; it is a little wooden pot with a lid that he turned on a lathe. We would spend the rest of the day with them, playing games and eating Christmas dinner in the Boys dining room. We would return home at night. The next day, Boxing Day, we had our home Christmas dinner.

The experiences that we had, with the patients and the staff at the hospital, were unique. It gave us a perspective on life, which we could not have received in any school. I believe it is probably the main reason I became a nurse, though from as early as I can remember, that is what I wanted to be. Maybe it taught me to be more compassionate and understanding of patients, and the difficulties they have to learn to live with. At the same time, what can be accomplished with time and hard work, towards living an independent and productive life, even with many great obstacles.

Chapter 13
Shadow - a Border collie of Distinction

The second year we were living in Oxford, we had an addition to our family, that gave many people, besides us, much joy throughout the years, especially when the family moved back to Aynhoe. One of our many trips home, especially after Mum and Dad got the family a car, was to bring back with us a puppy. We kids were told to go down to College Farm to look at their Border collie pups. There was about six of them, all very cute, but there was one that was smaller than the rest and kind of a strange dark mottled colour. He had four white legs and a beautiful white chest and muzzle. We all thought he was the best one - Mr. Oakey said he was the runt of the litter. We didn't know what that meant. He told us that Mum and Dad wanted us to pick one out for ourselves. So, of course, he was the one we picked.

Shadow about 1960

We were able to take him home with us that day, and we all decided he should be called Shadow because of his colouring. Mum and Dad did the training, though they both said that he was so smart, he really trained himself. We never needed a lead on him, as he would walk beside us, and when we came to a road, he automatically sat down until we started to cross over. We never had to give him orders in a tone of voice that sounded like directions. All we had to do was talk to him, as if talking to another person, and he would do whatever he was asked. He sometimes gave his opinion about the request. If he was lying in front of the living room fire, one of his favourite spots, someone would say to him in a conversational voice, "Move over Shad you're blocking the fire". He would give you this disgusted look, grunt, then move over, but not too far, so he still had plenty of the heat.

By the time he was a little over a year old, we would play hide and seek with him in the woods. Mum would cover his eyes and count to a hundred, and then let him go to find us. In the meantime we have gone as far as we could run into the woods, and hidden up trees etc.

with the plans already made as to what strategy we were going to use, to get back home before he could catch us. None of us ever made it back without being caught. His job was to catch us before we got back; this meant he had to tag us. This was accomplished when he touched our ankle with his mouth or nose!

We would run as fast as we could, when we thought we could out smart or out run him, in his trip around the woods to find and tag us. He seemed to know where each of us was, and where and what diversion we were using. He never broke his stride when he tagged each one of us, and would come so fast, that he would be back at home base before we had got moving very far at all. He would be wagging his tail ready for the next go. What was great about this was, he was always it, and thoroughly enjoyed being it.

He was our great protector. Our parents could not hit us without putting Shadow in another room, otherwise he would go for them. If they were going to hit us, and they didn't think Shadow was around, we would call him and he would come flying over to protect us. Our parents always knew we were safe as long as he was with us.

Lt-Rt 1949 Hayling Island , June, Dawn, Norman Alsford & Shadow

We could train him to play just about any game we wanted to play. He was the same with the boys at the hospital, as he was adored by everyone he came in contact with. We even had people with pure bred bitches ask if they could use him to sire a batch of puppies. They just wanted his brains and personality in a dog for themselves. Shadow was always willing to accommodate, whether requested or otherwise!

Up at the hospital they had chickens, which they were teaching some of the boys how to keep and care for, so as to earn an income, possibly from working on chicken farms. One of their responsibilities was to make sure the chickens were put in the chicken houses at night. One big problem, with people who have had head injuries, is memory. Either they have none, it is limited, or it is what is called having a short-term memory loss. In other words, their memory retention is short, so they have forgotten what has been told them, anywhere from minutes to hours afterwards. This meant that every night, Dad would have to go up to the hospital to check on the chickens; invariably they were still out. He always took Shadow with him. He said Shadow would sit by the fence and watch Dad chase these stupid chickens into their house. This one particular night they were especially difficult. He looked over at Shad, and he said he had this look on his face that he thought Dad wasn't much better than those fool chickens. With that Dad sat down and said to him, "All right Shadow if you think you can do so much better, you go and do it." He said Shadow promptly went over to a chicken picked it up in his mouth and carried over and gave it to Dad. He said he did this until all the chickens were brought to him, and in the house. From that time on, Shadow was the chicken catcher.

Another routine he had, was to go on his rounds each day, to places he knew were good for scraps of food. He knew the times to be there, and the days they had the best food going. We did not know the real extent of his tours, until I started work at a neighbouring business close to home, and I saw him outside the kitchens. I went outside to tell him to go home; the

Norman and Shadow

people in the kitchen asked me if I knew him. I told them that he was our dog, and apologized for him bothering them. They told me he had been coming there for years. They really enjoyed having him visit, and for me not to stop him from doing it. So I called him back and told him it was ok to come there, just not to be a nuisance.

Years later, after we had moved back to Aynhoe, Shadow had gone up to the shop with Mum, and she had told him to stay until she came out. She went in to the back of the shop, to visit with Auntie Adelaide (Gran's younger sister). When she left she went out the back way to our house. She said she missed Shadow throughout the day, but she thought he was probably on the prowl. In the late afternoon, someone came down to the house, and asked Mum if she had left Shadow outside the shop. She said "Oh my god, I forgot all about him." The person said; so many people had tried to get him to leave and go back  home, but he wouldn't budge, so they thought it had to be one of us to come and get him to move. Mum went up and he came away just as happy as a lark. Mum said he must have been there at least six hours.

When we moved back to Aynhoe, Shadow was over 8 years old. By that time, they are generally considered to be much too old to be trained as a workdog to herd sheep. Mr. Oakey, who owned the farm where we got him years before, thought that with his exceptional intelligence he wanted to try to teach him to herd, and to have

Sophie Howe a nurse at HHH w Shadow 1950

Norman work with him. It wasn't very long, and he was working the sheep as if he had been doing it all his life.

One afternoon, coming back from the fields, Norman and Shadow were crossing over the road at an especially dangerous part. They were downhill from a very sharp bend. Norman said later he didn't hear a thing, and had started across when this car came flying round the bend. Shadow, in less than a blink of an eye, got between Norman and the car. It missed Norman, but hit Shadow and carried him some distance down the road. After he got away from the car, he started to run home before Norman could stop him, leaving a trail of blood behind him.

I was about to enter Gran's, when I saw Shadow coming up the road with what looked like mud all over him. I called to him asking him what he had been into; he just kept coming towards me. Then I realised it wasn't mud but blood. It was pouring from his right front and back legs. I grabbed him, got him down and tried to put pressure on his wounds to stop the bleeding. By this time someone came by and went for help. Norman got there and helped put the pressure on him. Gran brought us towels, to wrap them to help stop the bleeding. It wasn't long before there was quite a crowd. Then someone came with an estate car, to get him to the vets in Banbury 6 miles away. Norman and I rode in the back with him, wrapped him in blankets to prevent him suffering any more shock, and to continue the pressure on the bleeding sites. When we got to the vets he was expecting us, so someone must have called ahead that we were coming.

The vet didn't have anyone beside himself at his office, so I told him I was a nurse and could help. We took him into his surgery. After putting him on the table before he examined him, he went to put a muzzle on him. I told him; you won't need that, he wouldn't hurt you. He told me he was going to have to examine him, and treat him without anaesthesia, so he did need to muzzle him. I told him; if I tell him not to move, it is going to hurt but you are not to move, he won't. He didn't believe me, so he muzzled him. I told Shadow just what I had said, and told him I'll be here but you are not to move. The vet looked at me very skeptical, and then started to work on him. He did not move a muscle through the whole time the vet was working on him. He kept saying I don't believe this, I have never seen anything like it. I said, "I told you so."

What he found was, that both the knee joints in his front and back legs were shattered, the wounds were open and it all looked to me like just fragments of bones. I am not sure exactly what he did. I know we were there for at least a couple of hours. He seemed to be piecing or rearranging the bone fragments. He put powder inside the wounds. He wrapped them with thick dressings and put them both into splints. He said he would be out the next day to see him, and would probably have to come out daily for a while. Also that Shadow needed to be kept quiet and warm, to only get up to do his business, and then for someone to be with him. He was also to be fed very high protein foods, to help heal his bones and wounds, with lots of eggs and cheese type products. He helped us get him out to the car and again, said; that is one incredible dog you have there. I told him we knew that.

By the time we got home, the word had spread throughout the village that Shadow had been hurt. We got home to a crowd of people, waiting to find out if he was all right; the phone rang constantly, asking after him all evening. We told them what the vet said, and what we were going to have to feed him to help him heal.

The next day, and until the vet said he could go back onto regular dog food, we were brought a steady supply of eggs and cheese for him. It was nothing for us to get four dozen eggs in one day. Mum would tell them that he couldn't possibly eat all those, and they would say that we could use them for ourselves. They just didn't want him to run out.

We made a bed up for him, beside the fireplace in the living room, with a pillow for his head and a blanket to cover him. He really lapped this up. Every day he had a steady stream of visitors to come and see him. They would go into the living room and ask him how he was. For each person who asked, he would lift his head up off his pillow, and sigh and let his head fall back onto the pillow. So then they would pity him, and stay and talk to him for a while, and tell him everyone was praying for him. His expressions were something else through all of this.

The vet said his back leg had the worse injury, but he may get by with just a small limp. It took several weeks to heal, but eventually he was able to go out and visit his old haunts. He was still carrying his back leg up, and people would stop and talk to him and wish him well when they met him. We had a strong suspicion that it was really completely healed, but whenever he was around people he would hold his leg up. Our next door neighbour, Florry Upton, could see him coming up the lane before he saw her. This one day, she noticed him coming towards her house walking

Shadow mid 1950's

on all fours. When he got in front of her house, he held his leg up, looked towards her house for her to come out and say to him; you poor thing Shadow. But this time she came out and said; Shadow, you old reprobate, there is nothing wrong with your leg. I saw you walking on it just fine. He looked at her tossed his head back put his leg down and walked on by. That was the end of his limping.

Shadow lived until he was eighteen years old, loved by all and missed to this day.

Chapter 14
Aynhoe the Later Years

During the time we were living in Oxford, I made as many trips home as I possibly could. Occasionally all three of us would go back on our own and stay there, anything from a few days to a week. Other times it would be just June and I that would go there, but most of the time I went on my own. June and Norman went together once, but they did nothing but quarrel. Gran told Den to tell Mum to come and get them. When Mum got there, Gran said; she would have Norman and me together, June and me together, but never the two of them together again.

Going to Aynhoe, and spending my time with Gran and Gramp, was my life-line. These trips home were when I really got to know my grandparents, Denis, Alf and his wife Pat. I remember one time, Pat was ironing when I went up to see her, and I told her I had a problem with ironing men's shirt collars, as they always creased at the points. She showed me that, if one started from the points, and ironed to the centre on the collar, that wouldn't happen. It works like a charm, saving a lot of time and frustration.

George and Ada Parrish May 1958 he died 6 weeks later

Alf used to grow prize-winning dahlias. He developed some beautiful colours by cross-pollinating them. This also gave some huge blooms. He had a small glass green-house, and his garden was relatively small - only about 45 feet square. It was ideal for what he was doing though, because all but one of the four sides, had an eight feet high stone wall around it. On the other side was his garage - combination barn. This afforded full protection from the weather, and with the wall it created a warmer climate for him to grow his dahlias. Dahlias make excellent cut flowers for the home, as well as a show in the garden.

Pat and Alf couldn't have any children, which was a shame because I think they would have made really good parents. I used to feel sorry for Pat. She never really fitted in with the village people. Maybe because she came from London and would have preferred the city life. Alf had a very gentle and quiet nature, and extremely good luck. He often won raffles, even to the extent that he won a car.

Denis, the youngest son of my grandparents, was only 18 years older than me; he was definitely my favourite of all their sons. He promised Gran and Gramp he would take care of them all their lives, and never get married if it would stop him from being able to do that. He was a men's hair stylist, which is a lot different from being a barber. He had gone to London for his apprenticeship and returned after the war to live with Gran and Gramp, and to work in Oxford at a place called "Strange's". At some point years before, Mum had worked there too, in the women's department.

Denis worked there for many years, taking the train to Oxford and back each day, which meant either walking the country mile, or riding his bike to the Aynhoe train station. There were buses in Oxford from the train to the centre of town. Denis used to cut the men's hair in the village in the evenings or on Saturdays. He did this for certain ones right up until he died.

Denis was a very quiet person in those younger years. He would arrive home from work; ask Gran, Gramp and me what kind of day we had had. Then he would go and wash up, and by the time he came downstairs, Gran had his supper ready for him. His face would really light up, if she had a plate piled high with chips, and two fried eggs placed on top of the pile, so he could pierce them and let the egg yolk run into the chips. He said ' You know just how I like them Mam'.

That would be the extent of the conversation you got out of him. Then he would go out for the evening, up to the Cartwright Arms. He was a champion darts player, so he spent a lot of time playing in the darts matches. This took him to many pubs in the area, where all the matches are held.

He was a person that believed that, if you couldn't say something good about a person, then nothing should be said at all. He was very kind, gentle and forgiving. If you had an idea about something, he would never put you down and tell you; "No you should do it this way".

Instead he would say; "Yes that is fine, or that's a good idea, but you could do it this other way and that might work." It usually was the better way, but with his approach you never felt he was interfering, or making you do it his way. I hope I developed some of his tactics for myself.

Gran, Gramp and Denis used to teach me to play many kinds of card games. One that was a lot of fun was called Newmarket, and involved money. But they said it wasn't really gambling, because no-one kept the money, as the same coins were used all the time. They said gambling wasn't good, because it could take food from children's mouths. The football pools didn't count either, because it was such a small amount that was played, or it was just harmless fun.

The other game they taught me was Whist. They had whist drives in the village hall. Eventually everyone at home thought I was good enough to go to a whist drive with Gran. I was told not to expect to win anything, or even do very well. I was told that it just takes practice, and that no one will be upset with me if I don't do well.

I will never forget my first whist drive, I was nervous about it all. We dressed up in our best clothes to go, arrived in plenty of time to visit with others, and for Gran to explain this was my first whist drive. They all welcomed me, though they had all known me all my life; it was all very proper. They each told me that if I wanted any help, they would be there to help whenever I needed it.

I didn't loose all my hands, but most of them. Still everyone there just kept encouraging me, and told me that I was improving with every hand. I never felt inadequate, or that I was in the way. I did win a prize at that first whist drive; I won the booby prize for loosing the most games. It was a little red plastic bucket, which I was very proud of. In subsequent whist drives I did learn to play a lot better. I never got to the stage of winning any of the first, second or third prizes, but I never won another booby prize!

When I was fifteen, Gran and Gramp celebrated their Golden Wedding Anniversary. I saved up my pocket money (at sixpence a week, it took me a little while) and paid Dad to make them two square planter boxes for outside their front door. I also made them their Golden Anniversary cake. They are made just like the Christmas cakes but the decoration is changed to fit the occasion. The family all gathered for the celebration, and it was a very happy occasion.

Gran and I used to go to Banbury shopping together. We would take the bus in the morning, the one after the workers bus (we felt we shouldn't take seats from the workers, who were most likely going to be on their feet all day). We would catch the bus back, that ran before the one the workers caught coming home, for the same reason.

Thursday and Saturday were market days. We generally went on Thursdays if at all possible, because it wasn't as crowded. Shopping in Banbury, where the shops had a larger variety of goods than the village shop had, or any of the delivery people could have on their wagons, was the attraction. We usually had something to eat for dinner while we were there. Most commonly it was fish and chips, from the fish and chip shop just off of the market square. If Gran was buying anything in the shops, she would remind the shopkeeper that she was paying cash for it, so she expected her discount. I wish that practice were in place today! When she shopped in the market, it was even more fun, because she would barter with them to get a better price. She told me in the market you are never expected to pay the asking price. That was also the case in a lot of the shops.

Watching Gran barter came in handy when I started doing my own shopping, as it does put a spark into shopping.

It was during these visits home, that I believe a lot of my development took place. It taught me what I thought was the right way to live one's life, how you should expect to be treated, and how you should treat others. During this time I read a lot of Dickens, and some of the other classics. These also had a big influence on what I believed to be right and wrong. Out of them all, Jane Eyre was my favourite. I always said my first daughter would be called Jane, and she is.

Back Alf Parrish Norman Alsford, front Ada Parrish Norah Alsford at Lower Lodge

Gran and Gramp used to come to Oxford for the day periodically. They rarely came together though, probably because someone had to stay home and make Denis's dinner. If Gramp came to visit us, or if he was coming back on the train with us, which is the way we travelled between Oxford and

159

Aynhoe, we had to leave in enough time so that when we got to the station, we had an hour to wait for the train. You could beg and plead all you wanted, not to get there so early, but to no avail. He would just say you should never be late, and you should never keep anyone waiting for you. To be late for someone is the biggest insult that you can pay him or her. It means they are not important enough for you to be considerate of them and be on time.

The walks to the station were not wasted with Gramp, as he would point out all kinds of interesting things on the way. He would point out bird's nests in the hedgerows, or the different birds or animals. When we got to the station, we would have to look at the Station Master's garden to see what he was growing, and how the flowerbeds were fairing on the station platform. Of course, he would discuss whether or not he would have planted what the stationmaster had planted in that particular spot, or that he or the stationmaster had better luck with a special plant. I believe it was during these times, that I learned a valuable lesson, of how to talk and listen to older people and enjoy it. I know I gained more from him, than he ever did from me.

In 1954 the Squire, Richard Cartwright, and his son Edward, were killed in a car accident just as they were returning to the village, on their way back from Edward's graduation from Eton. Richard Cartwright ploughed into the back of a large lorry that had broken down, and had no lights on to show it was there. His wife was in the car behind. It was being driven by the chauffeur. They were carrying all of Edwards' belongings. Father and son were killed instantly. It was a sad time for the village, bringing a lot of uncertainty. This meant Elizabeth Cartwright, the squire's daughter, inherited everything and she was only about 16 at the time.

The final outcome of it all was, Mrs. Cartwright moved into the vacant Graham-White house, that is part of Friar's Well and one of their properties. She had it extensively renovated, and moved in there with Elizabeth. The houses in the village, all but a very few, were offered to the tenants to purchase for nominal costs. Nearly all of them were either purchased by the sitting tenant, or by the children for their parents that were living there. Elizabeth still maintained ownership of a few of them. Denis bought the house for Gran and Gramp. He said the price was very reasonable, though a little more than some of the other village houses because it was larger. He said the price was £125, which, of course, in 1956-57 was quite a lot of money. Gran said it was so nice to think they owned their own home. Gramp didn't think he would ever see the day.

Later, I believe Elizabeth leased the Park House for 99 years or some arrangement like that, to a housing association that converted all but the large reception rooms into apartments for retired gentry. This was really the forerunner of very high-classed retirement homes. The house is still open to the public, because a lot of the artwork and artifacts relating to the Cartwright's are still there.

Chapter 15
Oxford and Around

I hated Oxford, or so I thought. What I really hated was, that I was not living in Aynhoe anymore. To this day, I still have a difficult time admitting Oxford really is a beautiful city, with incredible opportunities even for the non-college people living there. My response to this day usually is; I guess it's 'ok.' My husband loves it, and thinks it is one of the most beautiful cities in the world. Now back to Oxford in the late 1940's and 1950's, when we actually lived there.

In those days the University was made up of about 36 colleges, some dating back to the twelve hundreds when they were founded. The architecture includes many stunning buildings. Besides the colleges and churches, there are the museums. At that time, the ones we knew about were the Ashmolean, and the University that included the Pitt Rivers. Parts of the University were also: The Sheldonian Theatre, the Bodleian Library and the Radcliffe Camera, plus Rhodes House for the Rhodes Scholars from America.

Culture, besides the college activities, included two live theatres. One was the Oxford Playhouse, and the other the New Theatre. As students, the school frequently took us to see performances they thought were educational. This is where we received our Shakespearian educational requirements. We never had to read Shakespeare in school. What was the point when we could see it as it was meant to be? My favourite was always "The Taming of the Shrew". Not Shakespeare, but my other favourite they put on regularly at the Playhouse, was "Charlie's' Aunt". The New Theatre performances were the Royal Ballet Company, Covent Garden Operas, and West End shows before they went to the West End. This was one of their try out spots.

Because, logistically, we were central to many historical sites, we tended to be taken to those to see the history for ourselves, rather than to just read about them. For example, if we were studying castles, it makes more sense to see the different types, and how they were built and used. The same with the studying of fossils. We went to Shotover, a hill on the outskirts of Oxford, where they were in abundance, and dug for them ourselves. The same thing applied to Roman ruins, dungeons, torture equipment, ancient mounds and burial sights. This makes education far more enjoyable, and it is easier to remember because of the impression it leaves you with.

The rivers are an integral part of Oxford. The name Oxford is derived from Oxen Ford, a place where the oxen crossed the ford in the river. Which river though, I am unsure. The River Thames runs through Oxford, but the name is changed for that short trip to be called The Isis. The River Cherwell flows into the Isis, just past Magdalen College.

Part of life in Oxford, is punting on the River Cherwell. I can't recall any one punting on the Isis. That tends to be used by the larger pleasure boats. A Punt is a flat boat, that allows for roughly 4 people to sit in it facing each other, and a 5th person to stand in the back of the boat with a very long pole. That is used to push, or 'punt' the boat along. This is accomplished by inserting the pole into the water, down to the riverbed, to give the leverage to push the boat through the water. There is one very important part of this process which, if not followed; the punter will end up in the water. This to the enjoyment of all that are watching. This frequently happens during graduation week, when the students are well lubricated with alcohol, and forget what they are supposed to do. To prevent this from happening, after inserting the pole and pushing off, give the pole a sharp twist to release the suction created by the mud, water and pole. If they don't, the boat goes forward; pole and punter stay where they were, until the pole goes down into the water, with the weight of the punter causing it.

The River Cherwell runs up close to where Hilary lived, to an area called Mesopotamia. This was a very nice area, and a popular place for Sunday afternoon walks. If one takes a punt up as far as this area, when you get to the far end there are some rollers, which you have to pull the boat up, to get to the upper level of the river. On either side of the river at this spot, were some swimming areas. The one to the right was called Dames' Delight, and the one to the left, that the river ran through, was called Parsons' Pleasure. These were nude swimming areas for men and women. It is obvious which was which by the names.

June was always trying to sneak into the men's section, instead of walking around. This section was expected to be respected by all females. She succeeded one time with great planning. She dressed as a boy, in an Oxford Grammar schools boy's uniform, including the school cap, with another boy. She was severely disappointed, there was no one swimming there!

Oxford is the centre for the hospital Oxford District. This means the top specialist, and specialty hospitals are located there. The district encompassed, at that time, all of Oxfordshire and a large portion of Wiltshire. There could have been other neighbouring counties included, that I am not aware of.

In the city there was the main hospital called the Radcliffe. Close to that was the Eye hospital, the Ear, Nose and Throat hospital and the Nuffield. This was the obstetrics and gynecology hospital. The Neurology specialty was located in the Radcliffe. The Churchill was built for the Americans during the war, and was located on the Old Road in Headington. After the war it became the chest hospital, as part of the district. Not far from there was the orthopedic hospital called the Wingfield, and the Tropical Disease Hospital - most of those cases came from overseas. The mental hospital was located in the village of Littlemore, on the edge of the city. I always thought the name was ironically appropriate, Littlemore Hospital.

The concept behind this method, was that the smaller outlying hospitals dealt with the cases that did not require the high specialty personnel and/or equipment. This contained the cost of multiple unnecessary purchases, of expensive equipment placed in each of the hospitals, and the costly need of staffing all the hospitals with expensive personnel. The area is such, that a person could be rapidly transferred to Oxford if it was required, for proper and needed treatment. The specialists did make monthly visits to the outlying hospitals, to see the patients for their follow-up visits if required. During some of those visits they also gave lectures to the nursing students located there. I have always thought, that this method made much more sense, than trying to service every hospital with all the equipment and personnel. Maybe that is why the cost of medicine is now out of line.

164

Chapter 16
The Year After School

After I had finished school at fifteen, I was still too young to start nursing school, so I had to find a job to support myself. Because I was good at maths, Mr. Simms, our maths teacher, thought I would do well in an accounting office. There was another girl in my class – Anne Day - and we were close friends. She was the same as me with regards to maths. I think he was instrumental in getting us both a job, in the same prestigious office. We were each assigned to different auditors to work with. Anne's auditor seemed very nice. The first couple of weeks they had work to do in the office. With the auditor I was assigned to, he struck me as kind of strange, in a weird sense of the word, and I felt very uncomfortable and scared around him. We had a job in a private nursing home to do, that was going to take at least two weeks to finish. I stuck it out, making sure to leave the building very quickly at the end of each day, to catch my bus. When I realized I was going to have to continue working with him, I gave a weeks notice, giving some lame excuse why I wanted to leave. I then added; it would be a waste of their money to train me, because in a year I would be going to nursing school. I was told that, if I didn't like nursing school, they hoped I would come back to work for them, because I had real potential. Anne told me years later; the one I worked for was really a very nice person. He just didn't know how to relate to people. From there, I got a job in a place called the Drug Store. It was owned by the same family, that owned the shop next door called Boswells, which, in those days, sold everything from furnishings to gifts, clothes and toys. The Drug Store was a pharmacy, camera shop, and cosmetics shop, all rolled into one. One did not have to go outside the building, to go from one store to the other. My job was in the most unlikely place for me - the cosmetic counter. I have never been one to wear much, if any, makeup. I enjoyed working there the first few weeks. The person I worked for was Cherry Granville. She was a few years older than me, but a lot of fun to work with, as was everyone else there. It was during those first weeks, that this new drink was brought into England - Pepsi Cola. We had never heard of such a thing, and there was an ice chest of them located as you entered the store. English people, in those days, would not have dreamed of drinking straight from a bottle, so there were always straws to use. I still am unable to drink from a bottle without getting spit in it. We consumed more than our share of this new drink. After a while I noticed, that whenever I drank it, I had a real sharp gnawing pain in my left shoulder. To this day, if I drink Pepsi, I get the same pain. I don't get it with Coke. My interest in it soon passed though, and other than those first few months, I rarely drink any of the colas. After a few weeks at the drug store, Mum decided she wanted a break from hair-dressing, and was offered a job there, as the buyer on the cosmetic counter. My life changed dramatically. For a fifteen year old to work directly with her mother, is not a viable situation. Mum used to like to flirt with the male sales reps, and she thought it cramped her style if I called her Mum. So she told me I was to call her Norah. I told her she was my mother and she was going to be called that! I was very stubborn on that point.

Well, things went down hill from there. I decided I needed to find another job, which was a shame because I had just received a pay rise. Even though half of the rise went to Mum, in addition to what I already paid her towards my keep. I had started there at £1-5s a week; I had to give Mum £1 of it. I had an increase of another 5 shillings. Half of that had gone to Mum, but I still 7s6d to myself. I was saving up for a winter coat, and a pair of shoes that would slip on, instead of the lace ups Mum insisted on me wearing.

I knew changing jobs was going to hurt these plans, but I could not take working there anymore. As it turned out, I did much better financially, and food was included for all employees. So I didn't have to spend money on my midday meal, or go without it as I had frequently done in the past. It was walking distance from home, so that saved on the bus fare too.

My new job, was working in the Accounting Department for the Potato Marketing Board. It was a government agency, dealing with the potato-producing farmers across the country. It certainly wasn't a busy time of the year when I started working there. So I asked them if I could help out in some of the other offices, which were having their busy time. They allowed me to do this, so I was able to get to know a lot of people there, in a very short period of time.

I was paid £2 a week, and after 3 months they increased it another 5 shillings. Mum got most of it for my keep, but with the rise I did have £1 a week for myself. As I didn't have to catch a bus there, or buy my lunch, I really did quite well.

Before I started there, I had told them I would eventually be going to nursing school, but that was all right with them. I had already told Mum and Dad that. They did everything in their power to turn me off of it. Telling me all the terrible jobs nurses had to do for people. It had no affect. Then Mum said I was too shy, and that unless I went out one night a week, and did not come home before 9:30 pm, I couldn't leave. I didn't go out at night, because I wasn't interested in what the other kids were doing, and I couldn't afford too much. To meet her demands, I used to go to the pictures at the Regal up the Cowley Road, because I could walk there. It usually cost a couple of shillings to get in. Then I would be home by 9:30pm.

Gran and Dawn 1959

During this time, I was contacting different hospitals that offered the pre-nursing education/experience. There was one in Wiltshire called Savernake Hospital. It was located close to Marlborough, in the Savernake Forest. I went for an interview there, and Dad came with me. I had my school testimonial, and letters from staff at the rehab hospital. I was accepted and scheduled to start on 12th March 1956.

The people at the Potato Marketing Board, had a farewell party for me on my last day there. They said; if things weren't as I expected, then to come back. They would love to have me back again working for them

I started my nurses training in Wiltshire as scheduled. In 1957 I transferred to the Horton General Hospital in Banbury, for my remaining five years of training. During that period, most of my off duty time, (not that there was much of it), I spent at my grandparents. Headington Hill Hall closed around 1958-59. They had run out of head injury patients from the war. Consequently, my parents moved back to Aynhoe, and built a house next door to number 32 The Lane.

Lightning Source UK Ltd.
Milton Keynes UK
15 October 2009

145012UK00001B/71/A